Children as Parents

Children as Parents

Final Report
on a Study of
Childbearing and
Child Rearing Among
12- to 15-Year-Olds

Shelby H. Miller

Research Center
Child Welfare League of America, Inc.

Child Welfare League of America
67 Irving Place, New York, NY 10003
Copyright © 1983 by the Child Welfare League of America, Inc.

Current printing (last digit)

10 9 8 7 6 5 4 3 2

Printed in the United States of America

Library of Congress Cataloging in Publication Data
Miller, Shelby Hayden.
  Children as parents.

  Bibliography: p.
  1. Adolescent mothers—United States—Longitudinal
  studies. 2. Mother and child—United
  States—Longitudinal studies. 3. Adolescent
  mothers—Government policy—United States. I. Title.
  HQ759.64.M54   1983   362.8'2   83-5284
  ISBN 0-87868-204-X

To the young mothers who participated in this study,
whose candor and concern for their peers made the research possible:
To all that they are and the best that they aspire to become.

Shelby H. Miller continues to be actively involved in child welfare research. Since *Children as Parents: A Study of Childbearing and Child Rearing Among 12- to 15-Year-Olds* was completed, Ms. Miller has conducted a secondary analysis of the data collected through the National Incidence Study on Child Abuse and Neglect. This analysis, funded by the National Center on Child Abuse and Neglect, focused specifically on the relationship between maternal age and the incidence, type, and severity of child maltreatment.

Ms. Miller is currently directing the Child Welfare League's long-term demonstration of education and support for teenage parents and their infants in six major metropolitan areas, with an extensive evaluation component. This project, funded by the Ford Foundation, is being carried out in collaboration with the Minnesota Early Learning Design.

Contents

Tables

Acknowledgments

This research study involved the collaboration of many individuals, each of whom contributed greatly to the overall endeavor. The liaisons at the 13 local social service agencies willingly cooperated by identifying potential respondents, reviewing the interview schedules, and offering transportation and private meeting spaces for the interviews. The site coordinators assumed highly important responsibilities by contacting the young mothers and enlisting their interest in the study, assigning the interviews, and monitoring their completion by the interviewers. The rich data obtained and the high rate of completed follow-up interviews certainly reflect their perseverance, determination, and commitment to the study. The coordinators' extensive knowledge of adolescent parenting acquired through decades of service provision, community leadership and local policy development, and sensitivity to the needs of young mothers and infants were invaluable to the Project Director. The efforts of the interviewers were also highly commendable. In addition to full-time employment or graduate study, they conducted interviews with patience, understanding, and true concern for the respondents despite the fact that long waits, missed appointments, and a variety of distractions in the interview sessions were common. My appreciation and gratitude go to all those at the study sites who have worked closely with me during the last 3 years, as noted in the following lists of sites and collaborators.

My colleagues at the Research Center of the Child Welfare League of America have also provided extensive support and encouragement throughout the study. The guidance and constructive suggestions offered by Mary Ann Jones, the Center's Director, have been particularly helpful. Anne Moore has been extremely diligent with the large amount of

Local Agencies	Liaisons	Site Coordinators	Interviewers
CHICAGO			
Booth Memorial Hospital—The Salvation Army	Carol Bryant	Mary Eaton	Mary Eaton
Catholic Charities of Chicago	Ann Abrams		Carrie Patterson
Chicago Comprehensive Care Center of the Chicago Child Care Society	Raymond Fannings Lee Ryan	Mirriam Rosen	Jeannette Bennett Debra Collum Celita Jamison Martha Kurgans Cathy Lipper
Children's Home and Aid Society of Illinois	Alice James	Bea Gordon	Mary Sladek Anne Replogle
Evangelical Child and Family Agency	Doris Wheeler		
CLEVELAND			
Catholic Family and Children's Service	Florence Hangach	Rita Shambach	Rita Shambach Barbara Holland
Children's Services	George Delmoro	Ellen Mayer	Ellen Mayer Barbara Holmes
Lutheran Children's Aid Society	Rev. D. Marshall Begley Rev. John Wisch		
Services to Young Families—Cuyahoga County Welfare Department	Mary Butcher	Mary Butcher	Mary Butcher Terri Ali Alice Cox Marci Hyman

Local Agencies	Liaisons	Site Coordinators	Interviewers
MINNEAPOLIS/ST. PAUL			
Children's Home Society of Minnesota	Roger Toogood Jane Bose	Mary Lou Gladhill	Erica Fishman Elizabeth Fossum Ruth Hiland Carol Rennerfeldt Mary Schilling
Hennepin County Department of Protective Services	Charles Hogan Ray Ahrens		
Ramsey County Department of Social Services	Wayne Fox Pablo Davila		
Seton Child Welfare Services—Catholic Charities	Mary Kay McNamara		

correspondence and numerous drafts of this manuscript. Janet Clogston, Eli Mayer, Julia Giordano, Shelley Fischer, and Meg Lovejoy also assisted me greatly over the years. I would like to express my appreciation to these colleagues and my other associates who have contributed to making this experience so highly enjoyable and intellectually stimulating for me.

Shelby H. Miller

Funding for this research study
was made possible through a grant
from the Department of Health and
Human Services (ACYF 90-C-1791)

Introduction: The Issue

Adolescent pregnancy and childbearing have become problems of major health, social, economic, and political concern. Although there have been decreases since 1970 in the number of births to teenagers and in the birth rate for this group, the decline in adolescent fertility has been restricted to married teenagers. Childbearing among unmarried young women has actually increased since 1970. In addition, fewer teenagers marry to legitimize their pregnancies. Long-existing differences in the fertility rates between blacks and whites have also diminished. The rates for blacks have been declining faster than those for whites, making unmarried white adolescent mothers more prevalent in the population than they previously had been [Furstenberg et al. 1981]. The number of adolescents who become pregnant and give birth remains alarmingly high, 570,000 in 1977 for women under 20. Tables 1 and 2 summarize the trends in natality for women under 20 from 1950 to 1977.

Public concern has also increased over the rise in premarital sexual intercourse among adolescents. The proportion of teenage females 15 to 19 living in metropolitan areas who had had sexual intercourse before marriage rose from 30% in 1971 to 50% in 1979 [Zelnik and Kantner 1980]. Most of this growth is attributable to young unmarried white women. The proportion of white 15- to 17-year-old females having sexual intercourse doubled during the last decade.

The pregnancy rate among all unmarried adolescents also grew, from 9% in 1971 to 16% in 1979. This phenomenon is partly explained by the increased rate of premarital sexual activity among all adolescents. Better use of contraceptives and changes in the availability of abortion in the 1970s help to explain why the fertility rate has not grown proportionately with rates of sexual activity and pregnancy.

**TABLE 1   SELECTED NATALITY INDICATORS FOR WOMEN UNDER 20.
UNITED STATES 1950–1977**

	Year						
Age	1950	1955	1960	1965	1970	1975	1977
NO. OF BIRTHS (in 000s)							
15–19	—	484	587	591	645	582	559
18–19	—	334	405	402	421	355	345
15–17	—	150	182	189	224	227	214
<15	—	5	7	8	12	13	11
BIRTHRATES (per 1,000 women)							
15–19	81.6	90.3	89.1	70.4	68.3	56.3	53.7
18–19	—	—	—	—	114.7	85.7	81.9
15–17	—	—	—	—	38.8	36.6	34.5
<15	1.0	0.9	0.8	0.8	1.2	1.3	1.2
BIRTHRATES BY MARITAL STATUS							
Marital (per 1,000 married)							
15–19	410.4	460.2	530.6	462.3	443.7	315.8	—
Out-of-wedlock							
(per 1,000 unmarried)							
15–19	12.6	15.1	15.3	16.7	22.4	24.2	25.5
18–19					32.9	32.8	35.0
15–17					17.1	19.5	20.7
RATIOS OF OUT-OF-WEDLOCK							
BIRTHS (per 1,000 births)							
15–19	—	142	148	208	295	382	429
18–19	—	102	107	152	224	298	344
15–17	—	232	240	327	430	514	566
<15	—	663	679	785	808	870	882

Sources: DHEW, National Center for Health Statistics, *Vital Statistics*, Vol. 1, 1955, 1960, 1965, 1970 and 1975; _____, "Teenage Childbearing: United States, 1966-1975." *Monthly Vital Statistics Report* 26(5) Supplement (September 8, 1977); _____, "Advance Report, Final Natality Statistics, 1977." *Monthly Vital Statistics Report 27(11)* Supplement (February 5, 1979).

Reprinted with permission from F.F. Furstenberg, Jr., R. Lincoln and J. Menken, eds. *Teenage Sexuality, Pregnancy and Childbearing*, University of Pennsylvania Press, Philadelphia, 1981, p. 3.

It is clear from the tables that although the number of births to younger adolescents is quite small in comparison to that for older teenagers, this group experienced greater growth in fertility during the period from 1950 to 1975, as well as a slower decline in recent years, than was true of the older adolescents. Birth rates for younger adolescents even increased slightly in the mid-1970s, while those for older teenagers were decreasing. Data from the National Center for Health Statistics document a 50% increase in the number of births for younger adolescents, from 26,380 in 1960 [NCHS 1962] to 39,076 in 1979 [NCHS 1981].

Although, as noted above, the proportion of all births to adolescents accounted for by younger teenagers is quite small, one must remember that these girls, the youngest of all mothers, are capable of bearing several additional children while still adolescents, and many do so. They are also more likely than their older peers to be unmarried at the time of delivery, to remain unmarried for at least several years, and to be dependent on their families and communities for financial support. The economic, educational, and social consequences of initiating childbearing in early adolescence, coupled with the added effects of subsequent children, can be extensive and far-reaching, perhaps lasting throughout the rest of the young mother's life.

Although teenage pregnancy and childbearing have been the focus of considerable research in recent years, little emphasis has been placed on age-specific differences within the period of adolescence. Only a few studies have been conducted using samples of younger teenagers, and most of these were based in hospitals, utilized small samples, and concentrated predominantly on obstetrical issues such as gestation, birth weight, and length of labor [Briggs et al. 1962, Coates 1970, Mussio 1962].

TABLE 2 BIRTH RATES AND OUT-OF-WEDLOCK BIRTH RATES FOR WOMEN UNDER AGE 20, BY RACE, UNITED STATES, 1950-1977

Age and Race	Year						
	1950	1955	1960	1965	1970	1975	1977
A. BIRTHRATES (per 1,000 women)							
15–19							
White	70.0	79.1	79.4	60.7	57.4	46.8	44.6
Black	163.5*	167.2*	156.1	140.6	147.7	113.8	107.3
18–19							
White	—	—	—	—	101.5	74.4	71.1
Black	—	—	—	—	204.9	156.0	147.6
15–17							
White	—	—	—	—	29.2	28.3	26.5
Black	—	—	—	—	101.4	86.6	81.2
10–14							
White	0.2	0.3	0.4	0.3	0.5	0.6	0.6
Black	5.1*	4.8*	4.3	4.3	5.2	5.1	4.7
B. RATES OF OUT-OF-WEDLOCK BIRTHS (per 1,000 unmarried women)							
15–19							
White	5.1	6.0	6.6	7.9	10.9	12.1	13.6
Black	68.5*	77.6*	76.5*	75.8*	96.9	95.1	93.2

* Rates are for nonwhites.

Sources: See Table 1.

Reprinted with permission from F.F. Furstenberg, Jr., R. Lincoln and J. Menken, eds. *Teenage Sexuality, Pregnancy and Childbearing*, University of Pennsylvania Press, Philadelphia, 1981, p. 4.

In 1979, the Research Center of the Child Welfare League of America received a grant from the Administration for Children, Youth and Families of the U.S. Department of Health and Human Services (DHHS) to investigate childbearing and child rearing by young adolescent mothers. This is the first study known to be undertaken with a sizable sample of mothers aged 15 and younger who were in contact with social service agencies either during pregnancy or immediately after delivery.

The major objectives of the study were: (1) to describe in detail this particular portion of the adolescent childbearing population, including prenatal and postnatal health histories; family composition and background; self-esteem; school status and attitudes; relationship with the baby's father; sexuality and use of contraceptives; knowledge of child development; financial status; use of community support services; help provided by the extended family; information needs and resources; and educational, vocational, marital, and childbearing aspirations; (2) to assess the development of the young adolescent mothers and the babies during the first 2 years after delivery to determine how young teenagers adapted themselves to early childbearing and to identify changes that occurred during that period in health care and problems, school status, child care arrangements, self-esteem, sexual activity and use of contraceptives, and expectations for the future; (3) to determine whether and in what ways younger adolescent mothers differ from their older peers, in order to make informed recommendations for policies influencing programs and practices aimed at the very youngest of all parents.

CHAPTER ONE

The Child Welfare League Study

SELECTING THE SAMPLE

To be included in the study sample, a mother had to

1. be younger than 16 at the time of her first live birth

2. keep rather than relinquish her infant for adoption

3. deliver her first baby between January and October 1979

4. be in contact with one of 13 cooperating service agencies in Chicago, Cleveland, or Minneapolis/St. Paul

These three sites were selected because of their sizable populations of pregnant and parenting adolescents, minority representation, numerous social service agency programs, and the proximity of the programs. At each location, all social service agencies providing help for pregnant adolescents or young teenage mothers were asked to be involved in identifying respondents. The cooperating agencies were:

Chicago	Cleveland	Minneapolis/St. Paul
Chicago Comprehensive Care Center of the Chicago Child Care Society	Services to Young Families—a Program of the Cuyahoga County Welfare Department	Children's Home Society of Minnesota
Booth Memorial Hospital—The Salvation Army	Catholic Family and Children's Services	Hennepin County Department of Protective Services
Catholic Charities of Chicago	Lutheran Children's Aid Society	Seton Child Welfare Services—Catholic Charities

5

Chicago	Cleveland	Minneapolis/St. Paul
Children's Home & Aid Society of Illinois	Children's Services	Ramsey County Department of Social Services
Evangelical Child and Family Agency		

The 3-year study began in January 1979. Under the supervision of the project director, staff professionals at each agency, in conjunction with the site coordinators hired for the study, scanned recent files and intake forms for eligible cases. In all, 275 mothers who met the sample selection criteria detailed above were identified. These potential respondents were sent letters under the auspices of the agency to which they were known; the letters described the research study and its purpose, requested their participation in an interview, and offered $20 as payment for their time. In the letters, the mothers were also assured that their answers would be confidential. Stamped postcards with the agency's address were included with the letters, and the potential respondents were asked to return them if they were willing to be interviewed. The signatures of both the young adolescent and her parents or guardian were requested on the postcard. If the cards were not received within 2 weeks of being sent, agency staff members or, in some cases, site coordinators hired for the study, made follow-up phone calls to elicit the cooperation of the potential respondents.

One hundred eighty-four mothers (67% of those identified as eligible) were first interviewed several months after giving birth. Another 5 who were contacted refused to be involved in the study, and 86 were identified but could not be reached after repeated attempts. The first interviews were conducted from June 1979 to January 1980.

About a year after the first interview, site coordinators tried to reach each respondent again, usually by phone but in some cases by letter, to request her participation in a second interview. One hundred forty-four of the original respondents (89% of the sample) were interviewed a second time, approximately 18 months after delivery. The follow-up interview took place between October 1980 and February 1981.

Twenty-eight respondents were not interviewed again because they could not be located (disconnected phones or frequent changes in address). Seven had moved since the first interview, and it was not feasible because of distance to attempt to interview them in their new homes. Three mothers refused to be visited again, and one was hospitalized when the second interview was conducted. One respondent's baby had been adopted by her mother and stepfather and the agency strongly suggested that no contact be made.

It should be noted that the respondents who participated in both interviews were far more likely than nonparticipants to have been attending school at the initial session. They had also tended at that time (although differences were not significant at the .05 level) to be more likely to express high levels of satisfaction with their child care arrangements, to be living with one or both parents but not with a stepparent, to expect to acquire a B.A. degree, and to have gone to special school programs in the past. The two groups did not differ in any meaningful way in self-esteem, perceived competency in child care skills, relationship with the baby's father, use of contraceptives, or their parents' or mother's marital status.

ONSITE PROJECT STAFF

At each site, coordinators were employed to assist the project director with the following activities: identifying the sample; locating the potential respondents; assigning the interviews, monitoring their completion, and checking them for accuracy; and serving as local liaisons with the cooperating agencies. There were 5 coordinators, 2 each in Chicago and Cleveland, and 1 in Minneapolis/St. Paul. Twenty-one interviewers participated in the data collection activities: 19 for the first phase and 16 for the second. Some interviewers also acted as site coordinators. Fourteen of the original 19 interviewers conducted interviews at both times. The interviewers were instructed not to see respondents with whom they worked directly in a one-to-one relationship. Most of the mothers were not known by their interviewers prior to the interviews (77%), but 23% had been seen by them at the agency or in parenting classes or in groups of three or more at school. Efforts were made to have the same interviewer conduct both interview sessions with a respondent; 68% of the mothers interviewed twice had the same interviewer each time.

Most of the onsite staff held advanced degrees in social work, and all had had previous experience with young adolescents in medical, educational, or social service settings. Many were currently employed as social workers, teachers, or directors of comprehensive programs for pregnant teenagers and young parents.

THE INTERVIEW

Structured interview formats were used at both sessions.* The majority of the questions asked had only a limited number of response categories, but some questions were open-ended to elicit full expressions of opinion or to probe for possible explanations to previous answers. A self-esteem questionnaire composed predominantly of items taken from Rosenberg's [1965] *Self-Esteem Scale* and Coopersmith's [1967] *Self-Esteem Inventory* was administered halfway through each interview. The *Knowledge Scale* [Epstein 1980],

---

* Copies of the interview schedules (I and II) are available from Shelby Miller, Research Center, CWLA, 67 Irving Pl., New York, New York 10003.

a card-sorting technique developed by the High/Scope Educational Research Foundation to measure knowledge of appropriate expectations, was included in the initial session, and Alpern and Boll's [1972] *Developmental Profile*, assessing the child's functioning, was used in the second interview. The schedules were pretested with young teenage mothers who were participating in programs in New York City. Site coordinators and interviewers hired for the study were extensively trained by the project director before conducting the interviews. The first interview lasted just under 3 hours, the second, about 2 hours.

Place of Interview   More than half of the interviews (59%) occurred in the respondents' homes; nearly a third (32%) were conducted at the agencies where the mothers were known; and the remaining 9% took place at other locations, predominantly restaurants. Most of the respondents who were interviewed twice were seen at the same location for each interview (84%). The place of interview at both times differed significantly by site; more of the respondents in Chicago and Minneapolis/St. Paul were seen at home while more of the Cleveland mothers were interviewed at the agencies. The location did not vary at either interview by the mother's age or her current living arrangement.

GENERAL CHARACTERISTICS OF THE SAMPLE

Race   Eighty-five percent of the respondents were black; 11% were white; 3% were American Indian; and 1% were Hispanic. There were significant racial differences between the sites, as seen in table 3. Nearly all of the respondents in Chicago and Cleveland were black (90% and 91%, respectively), compared with 43% in Minneapolis/St. Paul. Because of the small number of white, American Indian, and Hispanic respondents, few comparisons among the various racial groups represented in the sample could be made.

The national statistics for births in 1979 for women aged 15 and younger show that 50% of all live births were to white mothers, 48% to black mothers, and 2% to mothers of other races [NCHS 1981]. The predominance of black respondents in this sample may be attributable to several factors: (1) the racial composition of the sites—Chicago and Cleveland having sizable black populations; (2) the sample selection criterion that respondents be known to social service agencies, thus eliminating some young mothers who were white, more affluent, and sought help only from private professionals; and (3) the selection criterion of studying only those who kept their babies. Currently, 90% of the unwed white teenage mothers keep their babies compared to virtually all of the black unwed teenage mothers [Alan Guttmacher Institute 1981].

TABLE 3 AGE AND RACE OF RESPONDENTS BY SITE AT DELIVERY

Chicago			Cleveland			Minneapolis/St. Paul			Total		
Age	Black	White & Other	Age	Black	White & Other	Age	Black	White & Other	Age	Black	White & Other
12 yrs.	1	0	12 yrs.	1	0	12 yrs.	0	0	12 yrs.	2	0
13 yrs.	5	0	13 yrs.	5	0	13 yrs.	0	0	13 yrs.	10	0
14 yrs.	34	3[a]	14 yrs.	13	3[b]	14 yrs.	2	2[b]	14 yrs.	49	8
15 yrs.	56	7[a]	15 yrs.	30	2	15 yrs.	8	11[a]	15 yrs.	94	20
Total	96	10		49	5		10	13		155	28

[a] Includes 2 American Indian respondents.
[b] Includes 1 Hispanic respondent.

Age at First Live Birth The respondents' ages at their first live births ranged from 12 to 15; the mean was 15.1 years. Sixty-two percent were 15 when they first delivered; 31% were 14; 6% were 13; and 1% were 12. The mean age of the 144 who participated in the follow-up interview was 16.1 years.

Marital Status Only two respondents were married when they were first interviewed. The rest had never married. One more mother had married by the time of the second interview.

CHAPTER TWO

Pregnancy and Delivery

THE PREGNANCY

Realization and Initial Reaction   Only 28% of the respondents realized that they were pregnant during the first month of pregnancy. Another 27% became aware in the second month; 21% said they knew it in the third month. The other 24% reported that they did not know that they were pregnant until sometime in the second trimester. The time of acknowledgment did not vary significantly according to the mother's age.

Only 11 respondents indicated that they had planned to get pregnant (6%). Pregnancies for the others were unintended (94%). When those mothers whose pregnancies were unintended were asked how they felt when they first determined that they were pregnant, most said they had reacted negatively (83%). Responses included: unhappy (38%) or sad (17%); scared or worried (24%); ashamed (3%); and "felt like killing myself" (1%). Another small group felt disbelief (4%). The remaining 13% had positive reactions, a proportion comparable to what Furstenberg [1976] found in his sample of predominantly older adolescents. Initial responses to the pregnancy did not differ significantly by the mother's age, when she realized she was pregnant, whether she had a sister who had been pregnant as a teenager, or race. This last finding regarding race opposes Williams's [1977] determination that blacks in his sample of teenagers receiving both prenatal and postnatal services were more likely than whites to regard their pregnancies favorably.

First Confidant   A third of the respondents (31%) first confided in their boyfriends when they discovered that they were pregnant. Another 27% turned to their mothers, and a sizable group consulted with other maternal relatives such as sisters (11%), cousins (8%), grandmothers (3%), and aunts (3%). Thirteen percent relied on friends, and the remaining 4% said that they did not seek out anyone. More of the respondents who had initially reacted positively to being pregnant first sought out their mothers, while more of those who had reacted negatively turned to other relatives or friends. Having a sister who had been pregnant as a teenager did not influence the choice of a first confidant significantly; neither did the age nor race of the respondent, nor when she became aware that she was pregnant.

Consideration of Abortion or Adoption A third of the sample (32%) indicated that they had considered abortion as an alternative to childbearing. Those who had initially reacted negatively to the pregnancy were more likely to have contemplated this option. Only a fifth of the respondents (20%) said that they had thought seriously about relinquishing the child for adoption. More of the whites than blacks had pondered this choice, thus more of those whose families had higher relative socioeconomic status. Williams [1977] also found that the white older teenagers (16–19) in his sample at the Rochester, N.Y. Adolescent Maternity Project were more likely than blacks of the same age to consider placing their babies for adoption. Historically, adoption has been viewed as a more likely option by whites, and despite changes in adoption trends, this still appears true.

Eleven percent of the total study population reported that they had thought about both abortion and adoption. However, past contemplation of these alternatives was significantly related to who the mothers believed would make important decisions about the child in the future. Respondents who said they would make decisions on their own were more likely to have thought about these options than those who planned to turn to others for advice. These independent young women appeared less influenced by family members in a variety of areas, and therefore may have been more willing to seriously consider possible alternatives to keeping the baby.

Consideration of alternatives to keeping the baby was not significantly related to the mother's age, when she realized she was pregnant, whether she had a sister who had been pregnant as an adolescent, or her attitudes regarding abortion. It is also worth noting that contemplation of abortion did not vary significantly by race or socioeconomic status, as did consideration of adoption.

PRENATAL CARE

Initiation of Care Almost all respondents received some prenatal care (98%). However, only 46% began care during the first trimester. Forty-eight percent did not begin until the second trimester, and 3% waited until the seventh month. Two mothers could not remember when they first sought prenatal care (1%).

A delay in obtaining prenatal medical services is not uncommon for women in general and adolescents in particular. About one-quarter of all the pregnant females in the United States currently receive no care during the first trimester of pregnancy [NCHS 1981]. Among 16- to 19-year-olds, nearly half (47%) do not obtain prenatal care in the first 3 months, and for those 15 and younger, the proportion is noticeably larger—65% do not initiate care until the fourth month of pregnancy or later [NCHS 1981]. It is worth emphasizing that the mothers in the study sample actually did somewhat better than others their age at arranging early prenatal care.

As might be expected, the timing of the first prenatal care visit was significantly related to when the mother realized she was pregnant. Most respondents obtained care soon after they confirmed their pregnancies. When the mothers were asked whether they had begun prenatal care at the right time, 60% answered affirmatively. Almost all of the others reported that they should have gone earlier, in the first or second months. The time when the respondent began prenatal care did not vary significantly according to her age, race, her family's relative socioeconomic status, or whether she attended a special school program during pregnancy.

Number of Prenatal Visits   According to the respondents, the actual number of prenatal medical visits ranged from 2 to 40, with a median of 11.6. Thirty-eight percent had 13 or more visits, thus meeting the approximate number recommended by the American College of Obstetricians and Gynecologists [1974] for a normal pregnancy. Another 42% reported that they had between 8 and 12 appointments. The remainder said that they went to a doctor or nurse fewer than 7 times, including three respondents who received no prenatal care. A few mothers could not remember how many appointments they had kept. As one might suppose, the number of prenatal visits varied significantly according to when in the pregnancy prenatal care was started, with more of those who began care in their first trimester having 13 or more visits. The number of visits did not differ in any meaningful way by the respondent's family's relative socioeconomic status or whether she had attended a special school program during pregnancy.

By the mothers' reports, they averaged more prenatal visits than the general population who received prenatal care (11.2) [NCHS 1981], black women of all ages (10.1) [NCHS 1981], and older teenagers (9.3) [Querec and Spratley 1978]. One explanation for these findings is that young adolescents are seen as a high-risk population. Once they initiate prenatal care many receive specialized services, including frequent medical visits, and are followed closely by health care professionals.

Seventy percent of the respondents thought that they had obtained an adequate number of prenatal care visits; 19% believed that they should have gone for more visits; and the remaining 9% indicated that they could have seen doctors less frequently.

Sources of Prenatal Care   Hospital-based clinics (50%) and public clinics such as those sponsored by the city's board of health (35%) were used by most of the respondents who obtained prenatal care, often in conjunction with the special school programs they were attending. Most of the other respondents saw private doctors. The white girls were far more likely to have obtained prenatal care from private sources than were the black girls.

THE DELIVERY

Gestation   Eighty-four percent of the infants were born after full gestational periods of 37 weeks, according to their mothers. The remaining 16% were premature (29), half 2 to 4 weeks early and the other half 5 to 8 weeks ahead of schedule. The prematurity rate for this sample was substantially greater than the 8.9% national rate for all births in 1979, comparable to the rate for the total U.S. black population that year, 16.1% [NCHS 1981], but much lower than the rate for those under 15 in 1979, 24.4% (28.2% for blacks, 18.7% for whites) [NCHS, personal communication 1981]. The lower rate for the study respondents may be explained by the specialized prenatal medical care that some received. However, one must remember that the findings regarding gestation are based solely on the respondents' reports. Length of gestation was not measured from the first day of the mother's last normal menstrual period to the date of birth, as is usually done.

Birth Weight   At birth, the smallest infant weighed 3 pounds, 4 ounces; the largest, 11 pounds, 12 ounces. The median birth weight was 6 pounds, 15 ounces, which was substantially lower than the national median for all babies born in 1979—approximately 7 pounds, 7 ounces—but identical to the national median for all black babies born that year [NCHS 1981]. Sixteen percent of the babies in the sample had low-birth-weights, defined by the U.S. Department of Health and Human Services as less than 2500 grams (approximately 5 pounds, 8 ounces) [NCHS 1981]. This proportion is much greater than the national rate of low-birth-weight babies born in 1979, 5.8% for whites and 12.6% for blacks [NCHS 1981]. It is also markedly greater than recent rates of low-birth-weight babies born to older adolescents, approximately 9% [Ventura 1977], and slightly higher than national figures for births to 15-year-olds (12.1%) and those under 15 (14.5%) [NCHS 1980].

   Birth weight was strongly correlated with length of gestation (r = .59). It is worth noting that the proportion of premature infants in the sample weighing less than 2500 grams was substantially greater than that among all babies born prematurely in the U.S. in 1979, 72.4% versus 40.6% [NCHS 1981]. The incidence of low birth weights among the full-term babies in this sample was 5.2%, in the NCHS sample, 3.1%. Eight of the 29 low-birth-weight babies in the sample were born after full gestation periods.

TABLE 4   DELIVERY PROBLEMS (N = 184)

Cesarean birth	12%
Long labor	4%
Forceps delivery	2%
Other complications (including birth injury, breathing problems, breech birth, and wrapped cord)	4%

Problems in Delivery   Seventy-eight percent of the respondents reported problem-free deliveries. The incidence of specific difficulties for the other 22% is shown in table 4.

The rate of cesarean births for the sample (12%) is somewhat lower than Placek and Taffel's [1982] figure for all U.S. deliveries in 1980, 16.5%, and their finding for births to mothers younger than 20, 14.5%. Significant racial differences were apparent in the frequency of cesarean deliveries among the sample, with more of the white mothers than black mothers having them (25% vs 9%, respectively). Of all U.S. deliveries, white women also have a higher rate of cesarean sections (15.6% for whites vs. 14.6% for other races) [Placek and Taffel 1980].

Length of Labor   According to the mothers' retrospective reports, length of labor ranged from 1 to 48 hours. More than half of the sample said they were in labor for 8 or fewer hours (52%). The median length of labor was 8.2 hours.

Relationship Between Prenatal Care and Obstetrical Outcomes   None of the variables concerning prenatal care—when the respondent realized she was pregnant, when in the pregnancy prenatal care was started, or the number of prenatal medical visits—were found to be predictors of positive outcomes of the pregnancy or delivery as indicated by length of gestation, length of labor, the infant's birth weight, or the incidence of cesarean deliveries. In addition, except where previously noted, the various outcomes were not significantly associated.

Length of Mother's Hospital Stay   Fifty-eight percent of the respondents remained in the hospital for 4 or fewer days, including time both before and after the delivery. Because Medicaid generally covers payment of only 4 days of hospitalization, this finding is not surprising. The mean length of hospital stay for mothers having normal deliveries was 4.8 days. This figure is noticeably higher than Placek and Taffel's [1980] 1978 average of 3.2 days for those having noncesarean births. As expected, the number of days of hospitalization was significantly related to the occurrence of cesarean deliveries, with those respondents having cesarean sections remaining in the hospital for an average of 10.1 days.

Early Separations   Sixteen percent of the infants did not leave the hospitals with their mothers following the delivery. Of these, most had medical problems such as prematurity, jaundice, or feeding difficulties that necessitated additional days of hospital care. Two mothers were contemplating adoption and did not take their babies home until they decided whether to keep them. The early separation rate of 16% is much higher than that found among married women of all ages, 7%, as indicated in the *1973 National Survey of Family Growth* and the *1972 National Natality Survey* [Bonham and Placek 1978].

CHAPTER SUMMARY

The average respondent in the study sample realized she was pregnant in the second month of pregnancy and began prenatal care soon afterward. Her initial reaction to the pregnancy was negative, and she first confided in her boyfriend. She did not seriously consider abortion or adoption as alternatives to keeping the child, although some of her pregnant peers did.

The typical mother had about 12 prenatal medical visits, slightly more than those received by the general population and substantially more than those obtained by all black women or older teenagers. Young pregnant adolescents are viewed as a high-risk population and, once recognized as such by medical professionals, most are given specialized services including numerous clinic appointments.

The average respondent was in labor for 8 hours and delivered a full-term baby weighing 6 pounds, 15 ounces. Her peers in the sample, however, were far more likely than all U.S. females—though comparable to black women—to deliver a premature baby. This finding is encouraging, however, considering the fact that prematurity is generally higher among babies born to young teens. The lower-than-expected prematurity rate for this sample can probably be attributed, in part, to the extensive prenatal care received by some of the respondents. The incidence of low-birth-weight babies among the young adolescents in the study sample was, however, far greater than that among all U.S. women and older teenagers.

Despite relatively extensive prenatal care, it would appear that a certain amount of negative obstetrical outcome for this population may persist as a consequence of age alone. The challenge remains for service providers to promote early initiation of prenatal care for all women through public education about the first signs of pregnancy and the importance of high quality medical care and good nutrition, as well as through the development of additional specialized prenatal care services for the very young. Only in this way will the negative obstetrical outcomes for younger adolescents be reduced further.

CHAPTER THREE

Status of the Mothers at Both Interviews

LIVING ARRANGEMENTS

First Interview   At the time of the initial interview, 88% of the sample lived with one or both of their parents. However, just 18% were residing with both parents; 51% lived with their mothers only, and 3% stayed with their fathers only. Another 14% were in homes with their mothers and stepfathers, and 2% were living with their fathers and stepmothers.

Of the 12% not with one or both parents, 9% were staying with other relatives, 2% were with friends, and 1% were in foster care or group homes. The respondents' living arrangements at the first interview did not vary significantly according to their ages but did differ by race, with a greater proportion of black respondents living with their mothers only (62% vs 22%).

Second Interview   Of those respondents interviewed twice, the percentage living with one or both parents had dropped from 88% to 81% by the time of the second interview. Ten percent were then residing with other relatives; 6% were in residential care, including 4% in foster family homes and 2% in mother/baby programs; 3% were in friends' homes. All of those in foster care were together with their babies. In total, 14% of those seen again were not in the same living situations they had been in when first interviewed. Most of the 20 respondents who had moved had left their parents' homes and were now staying with other relatives (5) or friends (5), or were in foster care (2) or residential treatment (2). Two mothers had returned to their parents' homes. More of the older respondents (17 at Interview II) and those who had become pregnant again had changed their living arrangements.

Later Separations   At the time of the first interview, several months after delivery, all the mothers were living with their babies except for one pair. That baby was in foster care then and was subsequently adopted. By the second interview, six respondents were not living with their infants. Two babies were in foster care and another had been placed for adoption. The other three infants were with their grandmothers while their mothers stayed with friends or other relatives.

One-fourth of the babies whose mothers participated in the follow-up interview had been separated from their mothers for a week or more by the time they were approximately 18 months old (24%). Thirteen percent had been away from their mothers for a month or longer. The most frequent reasons for separation were illness of the mother or child or second pregnancy or inability to handle responsibilities. The incidence of separations during this period was not significantly related to race. It is worth noting that Stevens [1980], in his research on black family social networks, has found child-keeping and temporary fostering to be very common among close female relatives and friends. The advantages of having a variety of caretakers who are eager to interact with the child and value the interchange are possibly reflected in the significant positive relationship Stevens found between a moderately dense network of female members and the infant's mental development as assessed on the *Bayley Scales of Infant Development* [Bayley 1969].

HEALTH OF THE MOTHERS

Postpartum Checkups   Eighty-nine percent of the respondents had obtained postpartum checkups by the time of the first interview. Almost all had returned to the same medical sources they had used for prenatal care. The other 11% had not been for checkups yet, but several of the mothers said they had scheduled appointments. Epstein [1980], among others, has also found very good use of postpartum medical care among the slightly older teenage mothers she studied.

Medical Problems   During the initial interview, 20% of the sample said they had experienced health problems since delivery. Most had minor medical concerns such as colds, and a few mentioned gynecological problems, primarily trouble with contraceptives. Problems at this time were significantly correlated with longer lengths of labor and hospital stays after delivery. Black and white mothers differed in the occurrence of such health problems, with more of the whites experiencing them (45% vs 17%). Five percent of the respondents had been to emergency rooms for medical treatment since the baby's birth. Eleven mothers (6%) indicated that they needed medical attention.

Almost all of the respondents seen for the follow-up interview had been to medical professionals during the interval between the two interviews (93%). Seventy-nine percent reported that they had gone for routine checkups; the mean number of checkups was 3.7. A similar proportion (77%) had seen a doctor or nurse specifically about birth control methods. The mean number of visits for this reason was 3.5. Eighteen percent had been to a doctor or nurse for other obstetrical or gynecological complaints. One out of four mothers said she currently had a health problem that needed medical attention (24%). These were predominantly colds, gynecological problems, and bladder infections.

At the second interview, 23% of the sample assessed their health as excellent; 44% rated it as good; 30% said it was average; and the other 3% reported their health status as poor. The mothers' assessments were not related to the number of medical checkups they had received during the period between the two interviews but were significantly associated with hospitalizations since delivery, with more of those who had been hospitalized stating that their health was average or poor.

Hospitalizations Fifteen percent of the respondents seen for the follow-up interview (24) had been hospitalized at least overnight within 18 months of the delivery. This figure includes seven mothers hospitalized because of a subsequent pregnancy. The other reasons for hospitalization were kidney infections (7); stomach or abdominal problems, including appendicitis (6); car accidents (2); and broken bones (2). A few respondents had been hospitalized more than once (3%).

Sexually Transmitted Diseases In the second interview, the mothers were asked if they had ever had a venereal disease. Ten percent responded affirmatively (14).

Satisfaction with Health Care During both interviews, all but a few respondents expressed satisfaction with the medical care they had received since delivery (98%); 48% said they were "very satisfied," and 50% answered that they were "somewhat satisfied." More than half of the sample had used Medicaid given with AFDC to pay for their health care.

SCHOOL STATUS

Eighty-five percent of the respondents were attending school at the time of the first interview or, if seen in the summer, had gone to school during the previous spring. Most of the 28 mothers not in school at this time had discontinued before their babies were born but planned to return in the next year. The major reasons cited for leaving school were the pregnancy and delivery, having to care for the baby, and disliking school. Those not enrolled tended (although differences were not significant at the .05 level) to be older and white, to have had health problems right after delivery, and to live away from parents or relatives. The two respondents who had become pregnant again by the time of the first interview had also dropped out of school.

Of the respondents interviewed twice, the proportion attending school had diminished substantially by the time of the second interview, from 88% to 69%. The actual decrease in school attendance during the time between the two interviews may be even greater than it appears, however, considering that mothers who were not in school at the first session were much less likely than those in school to be interviewed again (54% vs 82%, respectively). Seventy-two percent of the mothers who were in school at the first interview, and were seen again about a year later, were still enrolled, and six respondents who had not been going to school when initially visited had returned. It is worth noting that significantly more of the younger teenage mothers in this study sample were continuing in school at 18 months postpartum than were the older adolescent mothers in Zitner and Miller's [1980] sample.

Thirty-five of the 45 respondents who were not in school at the second interview had been attending classes when they were first seen, but the other 10 had not. A third of those who had been enrolled had gone to school for 7 months or longer after delivery before dropping out. As at the initial interview, two major reasons for school discontinuation were lack of child care and a dislike of school. The mothers who were not in school at this time tended to be older (17 years) and white, to have expressed some dissatisfaction during the first interview with the child care arrangements they had, and to have delivered a second child. In Cleveland the small number out of school was less likely than those attending school to have participated in special school programs for pregnant adolescents or young parents, as substitutes for their regular school. The school behavior of the Minneapolis/St. Paul respondents was not influenced by use of special school programs in the past. In Chicago, all of the respondents attending school at the second interview had been to special school programs during pregnancy or the immediate postpartum period. While the highly skewed distribution of special school program use by site makes conclusions difficult to draw, these findings do suggest that such activities can be beneficial to certain groups of adolescent mothers in terms of school continuation.

At neither interview did the mother's school status vary significantly according to her self-esteem or living arrangement, or the amount of formal education either of her parents had completed. School status at the first interview was also not influenced in any meaningful way by obstetrical problems such as low birth weight or prematurity or the mother's assessment of the infant's health status. In addition, school attendance at the 18-month follow-up session was not related to a recent change in living arrangement, the number of days of classes the mother missed between the time she became pregnant and was first interviewed, future plans she had for marriage or additional children, or the educational aspirations she expressed at the first interview. This last finding is just opposite to what Furstenberg [1976] found among a sample of slightly older adolescent mothers.

School Absences Nearly half of the mothers enrolled in school at the first interview (45%) said then that they had missed less than a week of classes since becoming pregnant. Another 40% had been absent for between 1 and 5 weeks during this time period, and the renaining 15% for 6 weeks or longer. The reasons most frequently cited for missing school were medical problems related to pregnancy (19%), negative attitudes regarding school (18%), maternity leave (16%), and other health problems or medical appointments (16%). Eight out of 10 of those still attending school at the second session had been absent for less than a month during the interval between the two interviews (77%). Again, illnesses and medical appointments were predominant causes of absences. At this time, lack of child care was also cited as a major problem by those who missed school frequently.

Special School Programs The response of many communities to increases in adolescent pregnancy and childbearing, as well as to the passage of Title IX of the 1972 Educational Amendments mandating equal rights for pregnant and parenting students, was to create special school programs. Most of these are under the auspices of the public school system and many are located in school settings. Some, however, are sponsored by social service agencies and housed at those facilities. A discrepancy among service providers seems to exist regarding whether it is preferable for a young pregnant adolescent or teenage parent to stay in her regular school or whether a separate, specialized educational program is preferable. Many special school programs offer both a general educational curriculum, as well as other relevant course work in child development, health care, and so forth. Others provide only the additional child care–oriented classes. Services such as prenatal and postnatal health care, counseling, vocational training and guidance, and recreation are often available at these programs or through referrals. According to a recent report issued by the Rand Corporation [Zellman 1981], the design of special school programs depends largely on the views of the prime mover in the community for such activities, and the school superintendent.

As mentioned previously, use of special school programs as a substitute for the regular school curricula was found to be significantly related to school status at the time of the second interview 18 months postpartum in Cleveland, although it should be emphasized that the number of mothers who had not been to such programs in the past was quite small. In Chicago, all of those seen for a second interview had been to special school programs. A much smaller proportion had used this service in Minneapolis/St. Paul, and their past attendance at special school programs was not an influence in school continuation at 18 months after delivery. School status at the first interview was not influenced in any meaningful way by past attendance at special school programs.

The nonmedical community services used most often by the respondents were special school programs for pregnant adolescents and young mothers; 86% of the sample typically had been to these during the last trimester of pregnancy and the first month following delivery. Those who were interviewed a second time were questioned about the number of months they had attended the programs before and after giving birth. The mean number of months before delivery was 4; after delivery, 1.2. More than half had attended both before and after delivery (58%); 30% had attended programs only before the delivery and 2% just afterwards. The other 10% had never been to special school programs. The positive program attributes cited by those using them were the chance to make up educational credits, being with others who were also pregnant or rearing young children, and the convenience of obtaining a variety of services at the same location. There were few complaints except for not being with regular classmates.

Significant site differences existed in the use of special school programs. Ninety-six percent of the respondents in Chicago had attended them compared to 83% in Cleveland and 48% in Minneapolis/St. Paul. Although special school programs were available for teenagers at all three sites, actual accessibility for individual respondents was not determined. The site differences can be attributed, in part, to the variations in services provided by the agencies to which the respondents were known. Some had special schools at the agency's facility or strong, well-developed relationships with the staffs of the local school programs, while others did not.

It is also worth adding that respondents who had seriously considered adoption as an alternative to child rearing were less likely to participate in special school activities than those who had not. Use of special school programs did not vary according to the mother's age, living arrangement, or which parents she lived with at the time of the first interview.

SELF-ESTEEM

An 18-item, self-esteem questionnaire was administered to each respondent approximately halfway through the first and second interviews. All but three of the items were taken from Coopersmith's [1967] *Self-Esteem Inventory* or Rosenberg's [1965] *Self-Esteem Scale*. Several of these items were modified minimally for use in this study. The items had both negative and positive desired directions and were arranged in order to reduce response set. Each item was answered on a 4-point scale ranging from "agree strongly" to "disagree strongly." The items and the distributions of responses for the mothers who were interviewed twice follow in table 5.

TABLE 5   SELF-ESTEEM QUESTIONNAIRE (N = 127)

	Agree Strongly		Agree		Disagree		Disagree Strongly	
	T1[a]	T2[b]	T1	T2	T1	T2	T1	T2
1. I feel that I'm a person of worth at least on an equal basis with others.	35%	32%	50%	61%	14%	6%	1%	1%
2. There are lots of things about myself I'd change if I could.	24%	26%	48%	50%	23%	23%	5%	1%
3. I'm a lot of fun to be with.	29%	32%	64%	61%	6%	6%	1%	1%
4. Other people who are important to me really accept me.	33%	26%	56%	63%	11%	10%	0%	1%
5. Most people my own age are more satisfied with themselves than I am with myself.	8%	7%	26%	21%	50%	60%	16%	12%
6. I feel I do not have much to be proud of.	2%	5%	11%	9%	55%	55%	32%	31%
7. I often feel pushed around by others.	7%	4%	19%	31%	57%	53%	17%	12%
8. I'm pretty sure of myself.	22%	20%	69%	70%	9%	9%	0%	1%
9. I'm easy to like.	24%	23%	66%	67%	9%	8%	1%	2%
10. I can't be depended on.	2%	4%	10%	11%	63%	59%	25%	26%
11. I'm popular with people my own age.	15%	11%	57%	64%	23%	23%	5%	2%
12. I certainly feel helpless at times.	8%	9%	55%	47%	32%	38%	5%	6%
13. Things usually don't bother me.	5%	3%	32%	36%	55%	53%	8%	8%
14. Most people who are important to me, who know me, think I do most things well.	22%	18%	63%	68%	13%	11%	2%	3%
15. I often wish I were someone else.	11%	3%	20%	23%	46%	53%	23%	21%
16. I would rather be supported for the rest of my life than work.	3%	4%	9%	6%	54%	51%	31%	39%
17. I am proud of my body.	16%	18%	62%	67%	18%	13%	4%	2%
18. The picture I have of myself in the future satisfies me.	26%	21%	63%	74%	9%	4%	2%	1%

Coopersmith items—2, 3, 4, 7, 8, 9, 10, 11, 13, 15

Rosenberg items—1, 5, 6, 12, 14

[a] T1—At Interview I

[b] T2—At Interview II

The overall self-esteem of the respondents interviewed twice was positive. A total self-esteem score based on a 4-point scale for each item was computed for every respondent at Interview I and Interview II. The possible range for the total scores at both interviews was 18 to 72. The actual range at the first interview was 33 to 68; the mean was 53. At the second interview the scores ranged from 32 to 65; the mean was 52.2. The correlation between the two sets of scores was moderately high ($r = .53$). The respondents' total self-esteem scores did not vary significantly at either interview by age, school status, living arrangements, or relationship with the baby's father. Neither were their scores at the follow-up session influenced in any meaningful way by the experience of another pregnancy. The total scores did vary by race, however, with more of the white respondents than black respondents having lower scores.

Despite the similarities in the distributions of the respondents' total scores at both interviews, the differences between their scores on individual items at the two times are worth emphasizing. The average absolute change was $+4.2$ points. Table 6 provides a more comprehensive description of the changes in the total scores over time.

The differences in the total self-esteem scores over time were not significantly correlated with any of the following changes that might have occurred in the mothers' lives during the interval between the two interviews: becoming pregnant again, being separated from the child for a long period, or changing living arrangements. Neither were they associated with the mother's living arrangement or school status at the follow-up interview, nor whether she had been helped by her family as much as she had expected before having the baby.

Although the total 18-item scale was highly reliable as an overall indication of self-esteem (Cronbach's α at Interview I $= .80$; at Interview II $= .84$), three major factors emerged through the use of the factor analysis with the varimax method of orthogonal rotation at both interview times [Nie et al. 1975]. The variables comprising the three factors are displayed in table 7.

TABLE 6 CHANGE IN TOTAL SELF-ESTEEM SCORES BETWEEN INTERVIEW I AND INTERVIEW II (N = 127)

Decrease in Self-Esteem of	
16 to 20 points	2%
11 to 15 points	1%
6 to 10 points	11%
1 to 5 points	37%
No Change in Self-Esteem	13%
Increase in Self-Esteem of	
1 to 5 points	30%
6 to 10 points	16%

TABLE 7   SELF-ESTEEM FACTORS[a] (N = 172) (ITEM NUMBERS REFER TO ORDER ON ORIGINAL QUESTIONNAIRE)

Factor 1 Self-Worth/Acceptance/ Popularity[b]	Factor 2 Manipulation/ Victimization[b]	Factor 3 Social Comparison[b]
1. I feel that I'm a person of worth at least on an equal basis with others.	6. I feel I do not have much to be proud of.	5. Most people my own age are more satisfied with themselves than I am with myself.
3. I'm a lot of fun to be with.	7. I often feel pushed around by others.	
4. Other people who are important to me really accept me.	12. I certainly feel helpless at times.	6. I feel I do not have much to be proud of.
8. I'm pretty sure of myself.	15. I often wish I were someone else.	11. I'm popular with people my own age.
9. I'm easy to like.	16. I would rather be supported for the rest of my life than work.	
11. I'm popular with people my own age.		
14. Most people who are important to me, who know me, think I do most things well.		
18. The picture I have of myself in the future satisfies me.		

[a] Using the procedure principal factoring with iterations.

[b] Factors named by the Project Director.

The first factor that accounts for 67% of the variance in the total self-esteem scores explained by the factor analytic solution appears to be an indicator of the respondent's positive feelings of self-worth, acceptance, and popularity. The second seems to be a general measure of attitudes regarding manipulation and victimization by others. This was comprised entirely of items that were negatively worded. Most of the respondents did not share these feelings. Twenty-one percent of the variance explained by the factor analytic solution is attributable to the second factor. The third factor is an indication of social comparison, self-worth as compared with peers. In addition to believing that they are popular and accepted by others, the mothers value themselves as highly as they think people their age appraise themselves. The other 12% of the explained variance is attributable to this factor. It should be noted that by far the strongest item in the third factor is number 5 ("Most people my own age are more satisfied with themselves than I am with myself").

The emergence of these three factors is not surprising considering the age of the respondents and the increased importance of popularity and independence during the period of early adolescence. Gordon [1972] sees the young adolescent as conflicted between the pressure to achieve and increased concern about being accepted by peers. Boys channel more of their energies at this time into the instrumental area (achievement and independence) while girls focus on the expressive area (interpersonal skills).

Three composite indices representing the dimensions associated with the three factors were derived for each respondent by first multiplying the factor score coefficient of each variable included in the factor by the standardized value of the respective variable (the mean of the variable divided by the standard deviation of the variable) and then adding these products [Nie et al. 1975: 487].

To determine what accounted for the differences in the respondents' self-esteem scores, the three-factor scores, as well as the total self-esteem score, were used in one-way analysis of variance procedures with other variables. F ratios at the .05 level were considered statistically significant.

Several meaningful associations were found between the respondents' total self-esteem scores at the first interview and other variables. In some cases, one or more of the three-factor indices scores from that time were also significantly related to the same variables. Although the causal directions of these associations are unknown, the relationships are still important to mention for those involved in service provision and planning for pregnant adolescents and teenage parents.

Higher scores on the total self-esteem scale were significantly related to the following: higher educational aspirations, satisfaction with the child care arrangement, high level of perceived competence at a variety of child care tasks, and a positive assessment of the baby's health status. Higher educational aspirations were strongly associated with all three indices representing the self-esteem factors. Satisfaction with the child care arrangement was significantly related to only one of these: manipulation/victimization.

In addition to being strongly associated with their educational expectations, the respondents' scores on the factor measuring self-acceptance and popularity were also significantly related to two other variables: frequency of contact with the baby's father during pregnancy and the persons involved in making important decisions regarding the baby. Those who had visited often with the baby's father during pregnancy or said they would consult with them or their own mothers when making important decisions regarding the baby, were more likely to say that they felt popular and accepted by others than those who did not do these things.

The mothers' scores on the index representing the third factor, social comparison, were also related to several other variables as well as to educational aspirations. Respondents who had no one else helping them with child care had lower scores, as did those whose parents had never been married to each other and those who did not use any method of contraception.

Overall Happiness During the follow-up interview, the respondents were asked to assess their general level of happiness. The possible scores ranged from 0 (completely unhappy) to 100 (completely happy); the median for this sample was 76. As would be expected, the mothers' ratings were strongly correlated in a positive direction with their scores on the self-esteem questionnaire. Respondents who said they had received more or about as much help from their families as they had anticipated before the birth were also more likely to give higher scores when appraising their current state of happiness than were those who reported that their families had not helped them as much as they had expected. The mothers' assessments regarding their overall happiness were not significantly related to any of the following: school status, number of hours each day the baby was cared for by someone else, current living arrangement, recent changes in living situation, or the experience of a subsequent pregnancy.

The mothers were also questioned at the same time about their current state of happiness as compared with their feelings 2 or 3 years ago. Nearly a third reported that they were happier now than they had been (30%); another third said they had been happier in the past (31%); and the remaining third indicated that their feelings were about the same at both times (39%). The dominant reasons given for being happier now were that having the baby gave the mother a sense of purpose in life and had taken her away from undesirable activities (i.e., being out on the streets, fighting, drugs), and that her relationships with close family members had improved. The main explanations given by the group who felt that their situations were worse than before were the tremendous responsibilities of bringing up a child (bills, constant care and supervision) and the consequent lack of freedom compared to what they had previously experienced.

CHAPTER SUMMARY

The average respondent in the study sample was living with her mother but not with her father at the time of the first interview and continued to stay in the same arrangement throughout the first 18 months after delivery. She had obtained a postpartum checkup during the first few months following her baby's birth and had also had four general medical checkups and three visits to a doctor specifically for contraceptives by the time of the second interview, when her child was about a year and a half old. Overall, she was satisfied with the health care she had received.

The typical mother was attending school at the first interview several months after delivery, but had been absent for a few weeks since she became pregnant because of medical appointments and pregnancy-related health problems. While she was still enrolled in school at 18 months postpartum, many of her peers were not. The mothers who had dropped out of school within a year and a half of delivery tended to be older and white, to have been dissatisfied with the child care arrangements they had at the first interview, and to have had subsequent pregnancies, carried them to term, and kept the baby. School continuation for the total sample was not significantly related to whom the mother lived with, her self-esteem, or the educational expectations she had expressed when she was first seen for an interview. The average respondent's self-esteem was moderately high at both interview sessions, and changed only slightly over time.

CHAPTER FOUR
Sexuality and the Use of Contraception

SEXUAL ACTIVITY

Age at First Intercourse   The respondents seen for the initial interview were 9 to 15 years old when they first had sexual intercourse. Their mean age at that time was 13.3 years. As one might expect because of the nature of the sample, this average is much younger than Zelnik and Kantner's [1980] recent figure for young women in general—approximately 16.4 years for whites and 15.5 years for blacks.

The differences between the white and black mothers in the sample in the onset of sexual activity were not statistically significant. The mean age for blacks was 13.3 years, for whites 13.5 years. Neither was age at first intercourse correlated in any meaningful way with the age at which the respondent had been told of methods to prevent pregnancy, her mother's age at the birth of her first child, or her family's socioeconomic status relative to that of the others in the sample. Most of the respondents believed that their parents were unaware of their having begun sexual intercourse. Parental awareness was not significantly influenced by the respondent's having a sister who had been pregnant as an adolescent.

Interval Between First Intercourse and Conception   The intervals between the mothers' ages at first sexual intercourse and conception ranged from less than 1 month to 59 months. More than three-quarters of the respondents had become pregnant within a year (76%); another 16% within 1 or 2 years. The other 4% had been sexually active for more than 2 years before becoming pregnant. These findings are comparable to Furstenberg's [1976] findings. Four out of five of the slightly older teenage mothers he studied became pregnant within 2 years following the onset of intercourse.

Present study findings can also be compared with those from Zabin,

TABLE 8   FREQUENCY OF SEXUAL INTERCOURSE FOR THOSE RESPONDENTS INTERVIEWED TWICE (N = 144)

	At Time of Conception	At Interview II
Every day	6%	1%
Several times a week	32%	20%
Once a week	20%	17%
1 or 2 times a month	20%	13%
Less than 1 or 2 times a month	22%	4%
Not at all	0%	45%

Kantner, and Zelnik's [1979] life table analysis on a subsample of sexually active women aged 18 and 19 from the *National Survey of Young Women*, conducted in 1976. Nearly one-quarter of that group became pregnant within a year of initiating intercourse (22%); 35% conceived within 2 years. The shorter delays for the younger mothers in the present sample can be explained, in part, by the sample selection criteria and the fact that young adolescents are less likely than older teenagers to begin to use contraceptives soon after their first sexual experience [Zabin and Clark 1981].

Frequency of Sexual Intercourse   The frequency of sexual intercourse for the respondents who participated in both interviews at two times of concern to this study, time of conception and time of the follow-up interview when the babies were about 18 months old, is displayed in table 8. It must be emphasized that just four respondents said that they had engaged in sexual intercourse only once before becoming pregnant; three of the four said their pregnancies resulted from rape. This finding is in opposition to some of the literature on counseling, which states that many adolescent unmarried mothers become pregnant as a result of one sexual experience [Chilman 1979]; in this study four respondents in all said they had been raped.

The respondents' frequency of sexual intercourse at the time of conception was much greater than that for the slightly older adolescent mothers in Furstenberg's [1976] sample. Two-fifths of the group he studied indicated that they were having intercourse as frequently as once a week; less than one-fifth had intercourse several times a week or more when they became pregnant. The higher level of sexual activity among the younger mothers in the present study sample may be explained by the general rise in sexual activity for teenagers during the decade since Furstenberg collected his data.

As the preceding table suggests, the respondents' frequency of sexual activity changed significantly from the time of conception to the time of the second interview. Sixty-five percent of those seen for a second interview reported that they were having sexual intercourse less often then than they had previously. Fifteen percent indicated that their level of sexual activity had increased, and the others said that they had intercourse at about the same frequency as they had at the time of conception (20%).

The respondents' frequency of sexual intercourse at the time of the follow-up interview differed significantly according to their future childbearing plans. Those who did not want additional children were less likely to be sexually active than those who did. The mothers' frequency of sexual activity did not vary in any meaningful way according to their ages, race, or living arrangements. Neither did it differ by whether they were still in contact with the baby's father or their future marital or educational plans.

EDUCATION ABOUT PREGNANCY PREVENTION

Nearly all of the sample seen for the first interview said that they had been told about ways to prevent pregnancy (85%). The ages at which they were informed ranged from 8 to 15; more than half knew by age 13 (53% of total). White mothers, on the average, had been instructed at a slightly older age than black mothers. Interestingly enough, however, almost a quarter of those who were told how to prevent pregnancy had been sexually active for a year or longer before they were given information. The age at which the mother learned about pregnancy prevention did not vary significantly by whether she had a sister who had been pregnant as an adolescent or her family's socioeconomic status relative to that of others in the sample.

Three-fourths of the respondents (74%) reported that since becoming pregnant they had also received sex education, predominantly at schools or in social service programs. This finding is similar to Zelnik's general figure for older adolescents: "Seven in 10 never-married U.S. women aged 15–19 have had a sex education course, almost all of them in school" [Zelnik 1979:355].

Only 12% of the mothers indicated at the first interview that they still needed sex education. Half of those expressing this need had previously attended classes on human sexuality. Twenty-three percent of the respondents seen for a follow-up interview said they wanted sex education. The lack of interest in sex education by the majority of mothers at both sessions is disquieting in view of many respondents' rather limited knowledge of the fertility cycle and their poor use of contraceptives.

Knowledge of Contraception   During the first interview, the respondents were asked to list all the pregnancy prevention methods they knew. Most were aware of the birth control pill (99%), the intrauterine device (IUD) (82%), and the condom (80%). Sizable proportions of the sample also mentioned foam, douche, or suppositories (68%); diaphragms (47%); and tubal ligation (32%). Rhythm (9%), abstinence (9%), withdrawal (1%), and vasectomy (1%) were named least often.

The mean number of different pregnancy prevention methods listed by the mothers was 4.3. This is similar to the number cited by both male and female teenagers in the New York City–based *Youth Values Project* [Ross 1979], but somewhat higher than that mentioned by the average teenager in Furstenberg's [1976] sample, who was slightly older. Respondents who had attended sex education classes were far more likely to name a greater number of methods than those who had not. The extent of the mother's knowledge regarding contraceptive methods was not significantly influenced by her school status, past attendance at special school programs, age at first sexual intercourse, whether she had a sister who had been pregnant as a teenager, or her family's socioeconomic status relative to that of others in the sample.

Knowledge of the Most Fertile Period During both interviews, the mothers were asked "Is there any particular time in the month when a girl is more likely to become pregnant?" They were asked to choose from the following answers:

- during the time of her monthly period
- midway between her periods
- just before she has her monthly period
- just after she has her monthly period
- yes, there is a particular time, but I don't know what it is
- no particular time

Table 9 displays the answers to this question for the respondents who were interviewed twice. It is evident that about 6 in 10 of these mothers had at least some idea of the fertility cycle at each time (56% at Interview I, 63% at

TABLE 9   RESPONDENTS' KNOWLEDGE OF THE FERTILITY CYCLE (N = 144)

	At Interview I	At Interview II
SOME KNOWLEDGE OF THE FERTILITY CYCLE		
Midway between her periods	19%	16%
Just before she has her monthly period	22%	23%
Just after she has her monthly period	11%	19%
Just before and after her monthly period	4%	5%
NO KNOWLEDGE OF THE FERTILITY CYCLE		
During the time of her monthly period	10%	5%
Don't know what it is	13%	12%
No particular time	21%	20%

Interview II). The accuracy of their knowledge could not be ascertained because of the way the question was worded. However, less than a fifth gave the most accurate answer at each of the interview sessions ("midway between her periods"). Presser's [1974] findings were similar in her study of females living in New York City who were 15 to 19 years old at the time of their first deliveries. Nineteen percent of that sample selected the answer "about two weeks after the period begins" as the time in the month when they were at most risk of becoming pregnant.

The limited knowledge of a large proportion of the respondents regarding the risk of becoming pregnant is obvious. Zelnik [1979], as well as others, has emphasized the difficulty adolescents have in assimilating this information, which calls for abstract conceptualization. In his study, only one-third of the 15- to 19-year-olds who had a sex education course covering the menstrual cycle could correctly identify the time of greatest risk of becoming pregnant.

It should be pointed out that the reliability of this question is somewhat doubtful since nearly half of the respondents (45%) were not consistent in the answers they gave at both interviews. A quarter of the sample (24%) had answers that were more accurate at the follow-up interview. Twenty-one percent gave responses that were less accurate, and the answers of the other 55% remained the same. It is clear, however, that most of these young teenagers were deficient in their knowledge and could use additional education regarding the risk of becoming pregnant, as well as other aspects of physiology and anatomy. This information must be given in a format that is age appropriate and at a time when it is most needed, well before initial intercourse takes place, preferably in the preteen years. For those who are already pregnant and planning to keep their infants, sex education should be provided soon after delivery.

Use of Contraception   Only 9% of the respondents who were interviewed twice were using prevention methods when they became pregnant, a much smaller proportion than Epstein [1980] found among the slightly older teenagers she studied (25%). Use of contraception had substantially increased by the time of the first interview, when 74% said they were using a method. The other 26% reported then that they were not using anything to prevent another pregnancy, but the actual proportion of this group at "high risk" of becoming pregnant could not be determined since their frequency of sexual activity then was not ascertained. The types of methods used at the time of conception and both interviews are shown in table 10.

The kind of prevention first used by the study respondents appears quite different from that utilized by adolescents in general, suggesting that the sample is much more likely to be connected with family planning clinics. Zelnik and Kantner [1980], in the 1979 national survey of U.S. women 15 to 19 years old residing in metropolitan areas, found that 19% of the sample had used the birth control pill as their first method, 36% had partners who practiced withdrawal, and 34% had partners who used condoms.

Use of contraceptives at the initial interview was significantly related to school status, with more of those attending school reporting that they were using them. Respondents who saw the baby's father frequently were also more likely to be using prevention methods then, as were those who had higher self-esteem in the area of social comparison.

Use of contraception at the time of the first interview did not vary significantly by the age at which the mother had been told about pregnancy prevention, past attendance at sex education classes or special school programs, age at first intercourse, whether the respondent had a sister who had been pregnant as an adolescent, or the number of contraceptive methods known. Many of the respondents using contraceptives then had obtained them at the 6-week postpartum checkup or soon afterwards. The lengthy delay in obtaining prevention methods by many in the sample is not uncommon. Zabin and Clark [1981] found a median delay of 9 months after initiating intercourse for the 1200 never-before pregnant teenagers they studied who came to family planning clinics. More than a third of these girls (36%) arrived at the clinics suspecting pregnancy.

The proportion of the sample who continued to use pregnancy prevention methods had declined slightly by 18 months postpartum, from 74% at the first interview to 67% at the second. Another 18% said they were not sexually active then, although more than half of these mothers were still taking oral contraceptives or had IUDs. The other 15% were not using any form of prevention at this time, but most indicated that they were having intercourse one or more times a week, and they were therefore assumed to

TABLE 10   USE OF PREGNANCY PREVENTION METHODS BY RESPONDENTS SEEN FOR BOTH INTERVIEWS (N = 144)

	At Time of Conception	At Interview I[a]	At Interview II[b]
Birth control pills	3%	57%	46%
Intrauterine device	0%	9%	12%
Condom	4%	2%	4%
Other (foam, douche, diaphragm, suppositories, withdrawal, shots, abstinence)	2%	5%	5%
No method, sexually active	91%	26% (no method)	15%
Not sexually active	0%		18%

[a] Whether the respondent was sexually active was not specifically asked at the first interview.

[b] Excludes the five respondents who were pregnant at the time of the second interview.

be at a high risk of repeat pregnancy. The group at risk may be even greater than 15% because of the inconsistent use of contraceptives. Nearly half of the respondents (48%) who reported taking birth control pills at the time of the second interview said they sometimes forgot to take them. Thirty-eight percent of those who used methods other than the pill or the IUD admitted that on occasion they did not employ them.

The reduction over time in the use of contraceptives is a major concern, but it is not atypical. Furstenberg [1976] found an even more sizable decrease among the slightly older teenage mothers he studied. More than one-third in that sample who had started practicing contraception after the birth of their first babies had discontinued it within a year; close to two-thirds had discontinued it after 2 years.

The use of specific pregnancy prevention methods at the second interview differed significantly from that at the initial session, although half of the respondents who had been using contraceptives when first seen were still using the same ones. However, 20% had changed methods and 28% had stopped using any form of protection altogether. Respondents who had originally been taking birth control pills were more likely to continue with them than were those using other types of prevention. Most of the mothers who had switched had gone from using methods such as foam and condoms to more reliable ones, either the pill or the intrauterine device. Several respondents had changed from the pill to the IUD, and a similarly sized group had done the reverse. In addition, nearly half (44%) of those who had not been using any form of prevention at the first interview had started by the follow-up interview, most often with the pill or IUD.

It is somewhat encouraging that mothers who change their types of prevention or start using contraceptives several months after delivery select more reliable methods. It is also worth noting that more than a third of the respondents who were using contraceptives at the second session (25% of total sample) had been employing their current methods for 15 months or longer, and another 26% for 11 to 14 months. There was a significant relationship between the type of method and the length of time it had been used. More of those taking birth control pills had been doing so for 11 months or longer, while those with IUDs or other methods had used them for shorter periods. A third of those using contraceptives at the time of the follow-up interview said they had employed other preventive methods sometime in the past, predominantly the birth control pill (15), intrauterine device (6), and foam (4).

Nearly two-thirds of the 47 mothers not doing anything to prevent another pregnancy at the second interview also said that they had used a contraceptive method in the past, most often birth control pills. The most frequent reasons given for discontinuing were actual or expected negative side effects such as stomachaches, bleeding, blood clots, nausea, and weight gain. Two respondents stopped taking oral contraceptives when they became pregnant.

Use of prevention methods at the time of the second interview differed significantly by race, with more of the black mothers than white mothers using some method to prevent pregnancy at this time. It was not related in any meaningful way to the mother's age, school status, frequency of sexual activity, or the total number of children she planned to have.

During the second interview, most of the mothers said they were satisfied with the pregnancy prevention methods they were using; 58% said they were very satisfied, and 29% reported they were somewhat satisfied. The rest (13%) expressed dissatisfaction. The respondents' expressions of satisfaction did not vary according to the type of contraceptives they used.

Preferred Method of Pregnancy Prevention The respondents were asked in the first interview which prevention method they preferred and what they thought most girls and boys generally liked best. Their answers are displayed in table 11. The birth control pill was the mothers' most frequent choice as the method for themselves (65%), but a sizable group selected the intrauterine device (21%). The respondents typically favored the method they were currently using; 81% of those taking pills and 88% of those with intrauterine devices said these were what they preferred.

Most of the sample thought that other girls generally favored the birth control pill (84%), but fewer believed that boys liked it (53%). The method they thought boys preferred varied significantly according to the mother's age. More of the respondents who were 15 at the time of giving birth than those who were younger reported that boys liked the birth control pill (63% of the 15-year-olds vs 38% of the 14-year-olds and 31% of the 12- and 13-year-olds). The mothers who were younger than 15 at delivery were more likely to say that boys would rather no method at all be used (31% of the 12- and 13-year-olds vs 23% of the 14-year-olds and 10% of the 15-year-olds).

Effectiveness of Prevention Methods The mothers who participated in the follow-up interview were also asked which pregnancy prevention method

TABLE 11 CONTRACEPTIVE METHODS PREFERRED AT INTERVIEW I

	By Themselves (N = 184)	By Most Girls (N = 179)	By Most Boys (N = 169)
Birth control pill	65%	84%	53%
Intrauterine device	21%	9%	2%
Condom	4%	1%	27%[a]
Other	7%	4%	3%
Nothing	3%	2%	15%

[a] This finding leads one to wonder whether the concept of preference was understood in the way intended.

they thought was most effective and which was least effective. Sixty-three percent selected the birth control pill as the most effective method and 23% chose the intrauterine device. The remaining 14% thought that diaphragms, condoms, or other methods such as abstinence, foam, suppositories, and tubal ligation were best. Most said that the method they currently used was the most effective. This was particularly true for those employing birth control pills or intrauterine devices; 82% of those using the pill chose it and 94% of those with IUDs selected that method.

A sizable proportion of the sample thought that foam was the least effective prevention method (35%). Fourteen percent thought the intrauterine device was unfavorable and 11% rated the condom poorly. Another 8% said that using no method at all was the least effective form of prevention; 6% were negative about withdrawal and 2% about the diaphragm. The other 24% could not answer this question.

PREVIOUS AND SUBSEQUENT PREGNANCIES

Eleven mothers (6%) had been pregnant once before the pregnancy leading to the first live birth. Seven had chosen to abort their pregnancies and four had miscarried.

By the time of the second interview, approximately 18 months after the first delivery, 28 respondents had become pregnant again. (For one, this was her third pregnancy.) The 28 respondents represent 19% of those seen for both interviews. Thirteen had carried their pregnancies to term, delivered, and kept the baby. Seven had obtained abortions and three had had miscarriages. The other five were still pregnant when they were interviewed. Half of those who had become pregnant again said they had initially reacted negatively to this pregnancy. Fewer of the whites than blacks had become pregnant again (7% vs 22%, respectively), but this difference was not significant at the .05 level.

The frequency of repeat pregnancies for these young adolescents within 18 months of their first live births is similar to that seen among older teenagers. In Zitner and Miller's [1980] study of adolescent mothers who were on the average about a year and a half older, nearly a fourth had become pregnant again within the same interval. Zelnik [1980] found in a national sample of teenage women interviewed in 1976 that 15% who had a first premarital pregnancy conceived again within a year after delivery; 30% within two years. The subsequent pregnancy rate among the approximately 400 predominantly black mothers Furstenberg [1976] studied was even higher. About a quarter of that group became pregnant again within a year after their first live births, and over 40% in two years.

The incidence of repeat pregnancies among the respondents was not significantly related to their educational commitment as evidenced by their school status or the aspirations they expressed several months after the first child's birth. This directly opposes what Furstenberg [1976] found. Neither was the occurrence of a subsequent pregnancy strongly associated with lack of knowledge regarding the risk of becoming pregnant as shown by unfamiliarity with the fertility cycle, as Zelnik [1980] has theorized, or use of contraceptives at the time of the first interview. The factors that help to explain the incidence of subsequent pregnancies among older teenagers do not seem to be the same for those who are younger. In this study, respondents who did not have anyone else regularly caring for their children at the time of the first interview were more likely to have become pregnant again by the 18-month follow-up session. It may be that these mothers are more committed to the one role of being a parent and therefore want to continue having children right away. Lacking child care, they may also be more isolated from services and other contacts that might allow them options for roles other than being a full-time mother.

No significant relationships were found between becoming pregnant again and the mother's age, living arrangement, the extent of her contact with the baby's father after the delivery, or past attendance at special school programs.

ATTITUDES ABOUT ABORTION

The 144 respondents who were interviewed a second time were queried about their attitudes regarding abortion. Table 12 displays their opinions about the acceptability of abortion in certain situations. The mothers were more likely to agree that abortion was "all right" when the pregnancy resulted from rape or incest or when there were imminent health dangers for the pregnant woman or fetus. Fewer thought abortion was permissible solely because of the woman's marital or financial status, her age, the number of children she wanted, or contraceptive failure.

TABLE 12 PERCENTAGE OF RESPONDENTS AGREEING THAT ABORTION IS "ALL RIGHT" UNDER CERTAIN CIRCUMSTANCES (N = 144)

The young mother's health is in danger by being pregnant and having a baby.	86%
She has been raped.	80%
The baby's father is a member of her immediate family.	77%
There is a strong chance that something will be seriously wrong with the baby.	72%
She doesn't want more children.	44%
The pregnancy prevention method did not work.	39%
Her family's income is very low.	31%
She is a teenager.	28%
She is not married.	11%

These findings are similar to those of a 1971 survey conducted by Zelnik and Kantner of both never-married and ever-married women aged 15 to 19, and the *1970 National Fertility Study* [Jones and Westoff 1973, cited in Zelnik and Kantner 1975] on ever-married women younger than 20. Zelnik and Kantner [1975] concluded after reviewing both studies that the greatest tolerance for abortions was for those situations involving the health of the woman, pregnancy resulting from rape, and the chance of fetal defect— reasons viewed as beyond a woman's control. There was less approval for situations involving a volitional component over which the women had at least some control (i.e., economic or marital status). The respondents in the current study were somewhat more accepting of abortion for a variety of reasons (rape, child's health, low income, no more children) than were those in the earlier two studies, reflecting perhaps the general increase in acceptance of abortion that has occurred during the last decade.

None of the mothers' attitudes regarding abortion differed by their earlier consideration of abortion or adoption when they first became pregnant or the experience of a subsequent pregnancy. In only one area were their opinions related to their current use of contraceptives; more of those using a method agreed that abortions were permissible in cases of contraceptive failure. Those who were sexually active at the time of the second interview were also more likely to be accepting of abortion in circumstances where the mother's health was in danger. Black mothers were more likely than white mothers to agree that abortion was all right in situations of contraceptive failure or if a woman did not want another child. The two groups' views on other reasons for abortion did not differ in any meaningful way.

A scale was created to measure the respondent's overall acceptance of abortion by adding the number of affirmative answers she gave to the nine abortion questions. (Cronbach's α for this scale was .77.) The mean number of reasons for which abortion was considered permissible was 4.6. Five percent of the sample did not believe abortion was all right in any of these situations; 7% thought it was acceptable in all nine. There were major differences between the black and white mothers in their general acceptance of abortion, blacks being far more likely to favor it.

The respondents' scores on this scale did not differ significantly by any of the following: age, living arrangements, school status, self-esteem, whether they were receiving welfare, the type of contraceptives used, knowledge of the most likely time of conception in the menstrual cycle, whether they had experienced a subsequent pregnancy, past attendance at special school programs, or expectations regarding education or expected completed family size. Although the differences were not statistically significant at the .05 level, it is noteworthy that the mothers who had intercourse daily were far more likely than those who had intercourse less frequently to have strong positive attitudes about abortion.

An attempt was made to develop a guttman scale using the nine abortion items. Our hypothesis was that a cumulative scale existed that had a hierarchical order from the reason involving the least amount of volition or no volition ("least difficult" to agree with) to the reason involving the most volition ("most difficult" to agree with). Respondents accepting abortion in one situation would be expected to concur with all other situations considered less difficult to agree with. The ordering of the items for the scale corresponded with their frequency of agreement.

While no clear hierarchical order emerged, there does appear to be an underlying structure in the mothers' responses, as displayed in table 13. The respondents can be viewed as three distinct groups in their attitudes regarding abortion: the "reluctants," the "moderates," and the "permissives." The "reluctants" (23% of the total) agree with no more than two of the reasons considered less difficult to agree with and no more than one of the reasons thought more difficult to agree with, indicating very low acceptance of abortion. The "moderates" (40% of the total) feel abortion is permissible for more than two reasons considered less difficult to agree with, but no more than one of the reasons thought more difficult to agree with. The "permissives" (37% of the total) think abortion is all right for several of the less difficult reasons and at least more then one difficult reason, indicating a generally high level of acceptance.

The hierarchical property, agreeing with less difficult reasons first and then more difficult ones, is further indicated by the fact that no respondents endorsed several more difficult reasons while simultaneously endorsing two or fewer less difficult reasons. This implies that acceptance of many less difficult reasons is a precursor for acceptance of several more difficult reasons.

TABLE 13 ACCEPTANCE OF ABORTION (N = 134)

Number of Reasons Less Difficult to Agree With	Number of Reasons More Difficult to Agree With	
	0–1	2–5
0–2	31 (23%) "The reluctants"	0
3–4	54 (40) "The moderates"	49 (37%) "The permissives"

Reasons Less Difficult to Agree With	Reasons More Difficult to Agree With
Mother's health endangered	Number of children
Rape	Contraceptive failure
Incest	Low income
Fetal defect	Age—being a teenager
	Unmarried

ADVICE FOR THOSE CONTEMPLATING PREGNANCY
AND THOSE ALREADY PREGNANT

At the follow-up interview, the respondents seen again were asked what advice they would give a friend of similar age who was thinking about having a baby. The most frequent answer was "Don't do it (don't have a baby), it's too hard when you're young, wait until you are older" (57%). More than a fifth of the mothers said they would counsel their friends to first consider their abilities to be parents and the responsibilities involved (21%), and 10% said they would advise their friends to use their own judgments. Just 8% suggested becoming pregnant and having a baby.

Respondents who shared positive attitudes about abortion were more likely than those who did not to advise their friends not to have babies. The advice the mothers gave did not vary significantly by their own or the baby's age, race, how frequently they had intercourse, the experience of a subsequent pregnancy, or whether they had considered abortion or adoption in the past.

When questioned about the advice they would give to a friend who was already pregnant, the mothers' responses were very different. More than two-thirds said they would recommend carrying to term and keeping the baby (70%). Only 8% suggested abortion, and fewer advised releasing the baby for adoption (3%). The others said they would counsel their pregnant friends to think over all their options carefully and then decide for themselves, or to seek advice from family members or professionals (19%). Most shared negative attitudes regarding alternatives other than keeping the baby, and reiterated these when asked this question.

The respondents' advice for a pregnant peer varied significantly by race, with white mothers being far more likely than black mothers to suggest options other than keeping the baby. Their suggestions did not differ in any meaningful way by the experience of a subsequent pregnancy; past consideration of abortion or adoption; current frequency of sexual activity; or future aspirations regarding education, marriage, or childbearing.

It is clear from these findings that most younger adolescents view becoming pregnant and becoming a parent as two discrete events, two decisions to be made. Most agree that becoming pregnant at an early age has negative consequences and they would advise others to wait until they are older. However, if a teenager is already pregnant, a different set of decision-making criteria comes into play. Carrying to term and keeping the baby is then the preferred option of most young mothers. Abortion and adoption are not considered by many.

CHAPTER SUMMARY

The average respondent was just over 13 when she first had sexual intercourse, 2 or 3 years younger than most other girls. She had been sexually active for about a year before she conceived this baby, and usually had intercourse at least once a week during this period. She did not use any form of contraception, although she had been informed about ways to prevent pregnancy at age 12. When she was pregnant she attended sex education classes and, following the 6-week postpartum checkup, she began taking birth control pills.

At the first interview, the typical respondent could name four different ways to prevent pregnancy: birth control pill, IUD, condom, and foam. However, she did not know when in her monthly cycle she was most likely to become pregnant. One one out of five of her peers was aware of the most likely time for conception. The mother's knowledge of pregnancy risk had not improved significantly by the time of the follow-up interview at 18 months postpartum despite the fact that she was still sexually active then, although less often than she had been at the time of conception. She continued to take birth control pills a year and a half after delivery but admitted that she often forgot them. A sizable proportion of the others in the sample were sexually active then and not using any protection, and many of the mothers employing contraceptives did not use them properly. The numbers at high risk of a subsequent pregnancy are disquieting and deserve immediate attention from service providers and policy makers.

One out of 5 of the 144 respondents who were seen for a follow-up interview about 18 months after delivery had become pregnant again. Most had carried their pregnancies to term and kept their babies. Although the incidence of subsequent pregnancies among the study sample is somewhat lower than what other researchers have found among groups of older teenagers, it is still disturbing in light of the ages of these mothers and their potential for bearing still more children in adolescence.

The respondents continue, despite their experiences, to view keeping the baby as the most preferable option once an adolescent is pregnant, although most would advise a friend their age not to get pregnant in the first place. The two events, getting pregnant and deciding to keep the baby, are seen as separate decisions by the young adolescents.

CHAPTER FIVE

Sources of Information, Knowledge, and Expectations Regarding Child Development and Parenting

SOURCES OF INFORMATION ABOUT CHILD DEVELOPMENT AND PARENTING

The first interview included a variety of questions about the respondents' sources of information concerning child development and parenting. The results are presented in table 14. The respondents' mothers' and other relatives were their most common sources of information both before and after delivery. Reliance on them actually increased after the baby's birth. Formal sources such as parenting courses, social workers, and school and medical professionals were turned to by about half of the respondents before the delivery, and use of them decreased after the baby was born. This drop was particularly noteworthy for parenting courses and school professionals. Friends and neighbors were depended upon least often for information; they were used by only about one-third of the sample. The mean number of different sources employed before the birth was 4.1, and after delivery, 3.7.

Best Source of Information As might be expected, many respondents considered their own mothers to be the best source of information. Forty-nine percent selected the mother as the best source before delivery, and 55% chose her for the period right after birth. Thirty-six percent preferred her at both times. The next largest group chose medical professionals as their best source, 22% before delivery and 18% after. Eleven percent believed medical professionals were the best source at both times. In all, 51% cited the same best source before and after delivery.

When the respondents who participated in the follow-up interview were asked to whom they would go for advice or help about problems with the baby, 43% answered that they would turn to their mothers only. Another 24% said they would seek out their mothers, as well as the baby's father or

other relatives. Others said they would depend on other relatives (8%), professionals (8%), or friends (3%) for advice. A sizable number of these respondents thought they would not rely on anyone in these situations (10%).

The reliance of teenage parents on their own mothers for information has
also been emphasized by Sparling [1980] in his review of 15 studies
investigating how young parents obtain needed information. He calls the
mother's mother "the most universally relied upon information channel."
Sparling determined, as well, that some young parents are receptive to
information sources that, in fact, do not deliver. Many young mothers
identify doctors and nurses as preferred sources of child development
information, but other studies have shown that these professionals seldom
provide concrete help [Epstein 1980].

Need for Information   The mothers were questioned during the first
interview about 11 types of information they might have needed before their
infants were born: health care; feeding; discipline; basic care; coping with
the problems of young parenthood; safety; methods to prevent pregnancy;
public assistance; and cognitive, motor, and social-emotional development.

Ninety percent of the respondents said they had needed some information
prior to the birth. More than half reported that they could have used five or
more different kinds (52%), and another 38% listed one to four needs for that
period. Seven percent said they had not required any information then, and
the other 3% failed to answer the question appropriately. The most
frequently mentioned needs for the period before birth were for information
about coping skills (60%), social-emotional and cognitive development of the
baby (57%), methods to prevent pregnancy (52%), and public assistance
(48%). Four out of 10 mothers said they would have liked information

**TABLE 14   SOURCES OF INFORMATION ABOUT CHILD DEVELOPMENT
AND PARENTING (N = 184)**

	Used at Either Time	Before Delivery	After Delivery
Mother	80%	64%	75%
Relatives	68%	57%	61%
Social worker	63%	54%	42%
Nurse	61%	50%	42%
Doctor	59%	50%	47%
Parenting course	58%	52%	28%
School	52%	48%	26%
Friends	39%	31%	32%
Neighbors	28%	20%	21%
Other	12%	5%	7%

regarding health care, safety, discipline, and the infant's motor development. Baby care and feeding were cited least often by the mothers.

Current need for information was also assessed during the initial interview. This had declined from the time of the pregnancy, with 57% of the sample indicating that they presently had no needs. Child development and public assistance were the two topics on which the largest numbers of respondents currently said they needed more information, by 16% and 13%, respectively. Another 9% wanted information on how to cope effectively as a young parent, 5% on pregnancy prevention methods, and 4% on health care. Although information about child development was one of the most frequently mentioned needs at both times, the diminished interest in this topic after delivery is a concern, considering some mothers' inappropriate expectations, particularly as to cognitive and language development, and the fact that many were not currently involved in parenting education programs where they would learn about these matters.

PAST EXPERIENCE WITH YOUNG CHILDREN

Almost all respondents had had some experience with young children before their infants were born. Nearly half (48%) had taken care of babies in their own homes a great deal when they were growing up, and another 24% said they had sometimes done so. A sizable group also reported that they had babysat for children of other persons either frequently (55%) or occasionally (25%) before becoming pregnant. In addition, more than one out of four mothers (28%) said they had read extensively about parenting and child care during pregnancy or the first few months after delivery.

PARENTING CLASSES

Past attendance at parenting or baby care classes was also common. Seventy percent of the sample had attended by the time of the first interview; however, the majority attended them only before delivery. Just 24% had participated in classes both before and after the birth. Black mothers were far more likely than white mothers to have been to these classes at any time (73% vs 45%, respectively).

Only 13% of the respondents who were interviewed twice said during the first interview several months after delivery that they still needed classes on child care. By the time of the follow-up interview, however, the group expressing this need had increased substantially to 51%. The sizable increase in the proportion of respondents identifying a need for parenting education during the first year after the baby's birth, although many first-time mothers express such a need, is cause for some concern. It is clear that the classes provided prenatally do not fully meet the teenagers' information require-ments. This is not surprising, for several reasons. The first is that the mothers' need for information obviously changes as the child grows older.

New needs appear as others are resolved. Because of their cognitive and emotional immaturity, young teenagers may also have difficulty generalizing what they have learned prenatally to a situation occurring more than a few months later. Most service providers would agree that during pregnancy the young adolescent, although focused on the changing physical aspects of her body, is more concerned about her own feelings, others' opinions of her, and handling present demands placed on her than the future needs of her infant. The baby is not yet a reality, and most young teenagers are almost completely unaware of the changes in their lives that the child will bring about.

These findings, as well as others presented later in this chapter, lead one to believe that the prenatal period is not the most effective time for parenting education. The issues that should be emphasized prenatally are good medical care, nutrition, making decisions about keeping the baby, preparing for delivery, remaining in school, and planning for the first few weeks after the baby's birth. Parenting classes should be available soon after delivery on a continuing basis, preferably until the young child enters school. The classes should focus on all aspects of development (basic care, physical, cognitive, and social development) pertinent to the child's current age, as well as on specific problems about which the parents may be concerned. Young mothers may also need a source for accurate information between classes. A

TABLE 15   RESPONDENTS' ASSESSMENT OF THEIR CHILD CARE COMPETENCE AT INTERVIEW I[a] (N = 184)

	Very Good	So-So	Not So Good	Do Not Know
How good do you feel you are or will be doing the following things:				
• giving the baby a bath	70%	27%	3%	1%
• doing the right things when the baby becomes sick or hurt	53%	35%	11%	1%
• showing love and affection to the child	95%	4%	0%	1%
• choosing the right kinds of food to feed the baby	78%	21%	1%	1%
• getting the child to behave the right way	57%	28%	5%	10%
• toilet training the child	38%	38%	9%	16%
• teaching the child the things s/he needs to learn	64%	23%	2%	12%
• encouraging the child to speak well	69%	14%	3%	14%

[a] Rounding results in some totals not equaling 100.

volunteer-staffed "hot line" or public health nurse providing routine home visits may be necessary to ensure optimal development for both the teenager and her baby. These and other suggestions for service improvement are discussed further in chapter 12.

ASSESSMENT OF CHILD CARE COMPETENCY

During the first interview, the respondents were asked to assess their competencies in eight different child care tasks as either "very good," "so-so," or "not so good." As table 15 indicates, most felt very confident about their abilities. The mean number of "very good" answers was 5.2. The mothers seemed particularly assured of their skills involved in the routine care of the baby: bathing, feeding, and showing affection. They felt less competent in more complex tasks: handling a child who is ill or injured, toilet training, and getting the child to behave in a desired way. Epstein [1980] also found that the slightly older teenage mothers in her sample felt positively about their parenting abilities in a variety of areas.

The respondents' assessments of their child care abilities did not vary significantly by any of the following: their own or the baby's age, race, self-esteem, with whom they lived, how many hours each day the baby was cared for by others and who the predominant caretaker was, whether they were attending school or had participated in special school programs or parenting or child care classes in the past.

EXPECTATIONS REGARDING CHILD DEVELOPMENT

The *Knowledge Scale* [Epstein 1980], a card-sorting measure developed by the High/Scope Educational Research Foundation, was used in the first interview to assess the appropriateness of the respondents' expectations regarding child development during the first 2 years of life. Each mother was read 73 cards describing particular needs or abilities of infants or toddlers, including nutrition; basic care; and physical, motor-perceptual, cognitive, and social development. She was asked to sort the cards according to the developmental periods when she expected the need or ability to first occur: 0 to 1 month; 1 to 4 months; 4 to 8 months; 8 to 12 months; 12 to 18 months; 18 to 24 or more months. The intervals were derived from Piaget's [1952] substages of sensorimotor development.

Thirty-one percent of the respondents' answers on the *Knowledge Scale* [Epstein 1980] were "correct"; that is, the respondents gave answers corresponding to the normal range of child development. This proportion is almost twice what one would have expected on the basis of random choices, 17%. Fifty-two percent of their answers were "incorrect-late"; that is, they expected these behaviors to be acquired at a later age than what is considered normal. This percentage approximates that which would have occurred by chance alone, 50%. The remaining 17% of their responses were "incorrect-early"; that is, the young mothers expected the skills or behaviors to be mastered at an earlier age than is typical. This proportion is just half of what would have been expected by chance alone.

These findings contradict results from other studies indicating unrealistically early expectations of teenage mothers. DeLissovoy [1973] determined that many of the 48 teenage parents in his sample were unfamiliar with developmental norms, expecting behaviors at a much earlier age than is typical. For example, they estimated that most babies could sit alone at 6 to 12 weeks, as compared to 28 weeks, the approximate developmental norm. Some of the discrepancy between the findings reported here and others may be attributed to a bias toward incorrect-late responses in the *Knowledge Scale's* [Epstein 1980] construction, so these findings should be interpreted with caution.

The developers of the *Knowledge Scale* [Epstein 1980] also identified items for three subscales within the total scale to allow for investigation of the respondents' expectations regarding specific areas of infant skill and behavior acquisition. These subscales were: (1) Basic Care; (2) Physical and Motor-Perceptual Development; and (3) Cognitive, Language, and Social Development. The internal consistency of the two subscales, Physical and Motor-Perceptual Development and Cognitive, Language, and Social Development, can be considered satisfactory (Cronbach's α of .73 and .74, respectively). The third subscale, Basic Care, was not reliable but it should be noted that it had far fewer items than the other two.

The study respondents gave a greater proportion of correct answers (expecting skill and behaviors within the normal age range) on the Basic Care and Physical and Motor-Perceptual Development subscales than on the Cognitive, Language, and Social Development subscale. Epstein [1980] also found similar differences among the 98 slightly older teenage mothers she interviewed during the last trimester of pregnancy and approximately 6 months after delivery.

A possible explanation for these differences was suggested by the service providers themselves. They find the issues of cognitive development and communication difficult to teach, as well as hard for the young teenagers to comprehend, so they do not always cover them fully in child care and parenting classes. Many of the respondents complained that too much time was spent in these classes teaching tasks like bathing and feeding infants, activities in which they already felt competent, and not enough attention was directed to issues such as learning and discipline. Other family members and friends may also be better sources for information about basic care than about how children learn, since they may lack knowledge in this area. It seems that accurate, extensive information regarding cognitive development is not as a rule available from either formal or informal sources.

It must be pointed out that neither the accuracy of the respondents' answers on the total *Knowledge Scale* [Epstein 1980] nor their accuracy on any of the three subscales was significantly related to the current age of their infants. Instead, the number of correct responses differed by the age at which the behavior or activity was expected to occur for babies in general. The mothers were far more likely to give correct answers on those items expected during the first 8 months of life than on those expected later.

The number of correct responses a mother gave on the total *Knowledge Scale* [Epstein 1980], as well as the number of correct responses she had on the three subscales, was also not significantly correlated with any of the following: her age or her family's socioeconomic status relative to that of others in the sample, her assessment of her competency at various child care tasks, or past attendance at special school programs or parenting education classes. This last finding indicating the lack of a significant impact of special school and classes is not surprising, since the teenager's mother and other family members are her major sources for information about child care and development.

In this study, as well as in others [Stevens 1980], the adolescent mother's knowledge of child development has not been found to be a strong predictor of her infant's development when the child was about a year and a half old. The respondent's accuracy on the *Knowledge Scale* [Epstein 1980] several months after delivery at the first interview was not significantly related to her assessment of her child's performance at the follow-up interview 18 months postpartum, as indicated on the Alpern and Boll [1972] *Developmental Profile* (See chapter 6). A possible explanation for the lack of a strong relationship is that these infants are away from their mothers for many hours each day and their development is influenced by other adult caretakers. One might also suspect that the child's learning environment would have to be extremely deprived to result in substantial cognitive deficits at this early age.

The lack of a strong association between parental knowledge and the child's performance may lead one to question the value of additional parenting education. However, the deficits in cognitive and language development among preschool and school-age children who were born to teenage mothers that other researchers have identified lead one to recommend it. The classes would probably be most effective if they focused on specific concerns identified by the mothers, particularly in the areas of cognitive and affective development. Information should be directed to the children's current stage of development and to behaviors and skills they soon will be demonstrating. But dissemination of information is not enough. These young mothers have to know how to incorporate what they have learned into their daily routines and assume habits that will promote the child's learning. Although information about child development was one of the most frequently mentioned needs at both times, the diminished interest in this topic after delivery is a concern, considering some mothers' inappropriate expectations, particularly in the areas of cognitive and language development, and the fact that many were not currently involved in parenting education programs in which they would learn about these issues.

CHAPTER SUMMARY

The average respondent relied heavily on her family, particularly her mother, for information about child development and parenting. Dependence on the family actually increased slightly after the baby's birth. Social workers, doctors, and nurses were also sources of information for about half the sample of respondents during pregnancy and immediately after delivery. However, few respondents who were seen for follow-up interviews said they would seek advice from these professionals at that time. It may be that their earlier contacts with them were part of special school programs or the activities of social service agencies. Since so many of the services for young teenage parents terminate within a few months after delivery, the decrease in reliance on professionals is not surprising.

It is clear that the young mother's information needs and interests change after the baby is born and during the first few years after delivery. Although many respondents said they had no need for information at the first interview, the fact that some lack adequate knowledge regarding appropriate child development expectations and that half reported that they needed parenting education at the follow-up interview 18 months postpartum is evidence that they would probably benefit from additional classes on parenting, a supportive one-to-one relationship with someone who has been a successful parent, and extensive information about child development given at a level appropriate to their age.

Almost all the respondents had cared for younger siblings or babysat for other people's children before their own infants were born. Seven out of 10 had also attended parenting or baby care classes, mostly before the delivery. The proportion saying that they needed additional parenting education, however, increased substantially from the first interview to the second, from 13% to 51%. This increased need is a major concern, considering the lack of services for many teenage mothers once their babies are several months old.

During the first interview several months after delivery, the respondents were queried about their competence at various child care tasks. At least 7 out of 10 said they had very good skills in bathing, feeding, and showing affection, but fewer were confident about their abilities in toilet training, disciplining, and caring for sick infants. Some mothers admitted that they were not competent in certain tasks and others did not know how well they would handle them when the tasks arose. It is clear that at least 1 out of 3 of the mothers in the sample might benefit from training aimed at increasing their competence at child care skills. To date, however, the mothers' assessments have not been influenced significantly by their attendance at special school programs or classes.

The *Knowledge Scale* [Epstein 1980], a card-sorting measure developed by the High/Scope Educational Research Foundation, was also used in the first interview to assess the mothers' knowledge of appropriate child development expectations. The respondents were found to have more correct answers on the scale than one would have anticipated on the basis of random choice, and this is somewhat encouraging. However, many of their answers were incorrect and this fact, coupled with the findings that half reported a need for parenting classes and one out of three did not feel confident of their competence at various child care tasks, lead one to believe that additional parenting education would probably be beneficial. However, the connection between parental knowledge of appropriate child development expectations and the child's actual behavior remains unclear. Better ways have to be found to help young mothers learn about child development and transfer what they know into action.

CHAPTER SIX

The Infants

CHARACTERISTICS OF THE INFANTS

Sex There were 186 infants in the study sample, 86 females (46%) and 100 males (54%), including two sets of male twins. One twin died at 5 months of age. The cause of death given was sudden infant death syndrome.

Age The babies had been born between January and October 1979. At the time of the first interview, they ranged in age from 4 to 50 weeks, with a median age of 3.2 months. The median age of the 144 children whose mothers were seen for the second interview was 18.4 months.

As table 16 indicates, there were significant site differences in the age of the infants at the first interview, with more of those in Minneapolis/St. Paul than those in Chicago or Cleveland being 4 months or older. Thus, the white babies were somewhat older than the black babies when their mothers were first seen, since most of the whites lived in Minneapolis/St. Paul. These site differences were no longer apparent at the follow-up interview due to careful scheduling of sessions.

TABLE 16 INFANTS' AGE BY SITE AT INTERVIEW I

	Chicago	Cleveland	Minneapolis/ St. Paul
4 to 8 weeks	12%	22%	0
9 to 13 weeks	39%	32%	21%
14 to 18 weeks	36%	33%	22%
19 to 23 weeks	11%	7%	22%
24 to 50 weeks	2%	6%	35%
	(N = 107)	(N = 54)	(N = 23)

Health   At the first interview, several months after delivery, 55% of the respondents assessed the child's health as excellent, and 34% appraised it as good. Another 9% indicated that the baby's health was average and 2% thought it was poor. By the time of the second interview, many of those seen again did not appraise the child's health status as positively as they had previously, as can be seen in table 17.

The change in the mothers' assessments is not surprising in view of the increased prevalence of health problems among the infants during the interval between the interviews, discussed later in this section. The differences in the mothers' assessments at the two interviews, although worth mentioning, were not statistically significant at the .05 level.

MEDICAL CARE

Most of the infants (95%) had been taken to medical professionals within the first few months after delivery. All of those whose mothers participated in the follow-up interview had seen a doctor or nurse. Between the first and second interviews, 96% of these babies had had at least one checkup. Fifteen percent had one to three checkups during this period; 44%, four to six appointments; and 36%, seven or more routine medical visits. Two respondents could not remember how many checkups their children had received (1%). The number of checkups did not vary significantly according to the baby's age or how the mother had assessed the infant's health status at the first interview. The frequent medical appointments for some of the babies can be attributed, in part, to the fact that some service providers view children of young adolescent mothers as a high-risk population and give them numerous medical checkups when reimbursible by Medicaid, whether necessary or not.

Despite the findings that a large proportion of the infants had frequent medical attention and that the mothers generally held positive assessments of the child's health status, the incidence of health problems requiring professional care was surprisingly high, as table 18 on page 54 indicates. Half of the infants (51%) had experienced at least one problem by the first interview. A large proportion of the babies continued to evidence specific health conditions at the second interview, the most frequent being respiratory or bowel-related. It should be noted also that at the second interview an interviewer suspected physical abuse of one infant and a report was made to the proper authorities.

Recurring Health Problems   During the second interview, 53% of the respondents seen again reported that the child had health problems that kept returning. The most frequently mentioned was colds, by 33% of the sample. Eight percent said their babies often had rashes, and 4% identified diarrhea or constipation as recurring problems. It is noteworthy that in 23%

of the families both the mothers and children had persistent health problems.

Hospitalizations More than a fifth of the infants whose mothers were seen for both interviews (22%) had been hospitalized at least overnight by the time of the follow-up interview. The major reasons for hospitalization were diarrhea or constipation (7%), pneumonia or bronchitis (6%), and allergies (3%). Six percent of the babies had been hospitalized more than once.

Use of Hospital Emergency Rooms Twenty-two percent of the infants had been taken to emergency rooms during their first few months of life. Babies with respiratory, bowel, or eating problems were more likely to be taken there than those presenting other symptoms. No significant relationship existed between the use of hospital emergency rooms and hospitalization of the infants. Neither did use of hospital emergency rooms for the babies differ significantly by the respondent's family's relative socioeconomic status, her living arrangement, or receipt of public assistance. However, use of these facilities was strongly associated with a large number of housing problems, such as a lack of heat or unsafe conditions.

Immunizations Only four babies had not received any immunizations by the second interview, approximately 18 months after delivery. Most did get the polio, diphtheria, tetanus, measles, rubella, and mumps immunizations required at their ages, according to the respondents. The mean number of shots was five. Black babies were far more likely than white babies to have had five or more shots. The number of shots the babies received did not vary significantly according to the infants' ages or the respondents' current living arrangements.

Satisfaction with Health Care Almost three-quarters of the sample (71%) seen for the second interview reported that they were very satisfied with the health care their babies had received. Another 24% said they were somewhat satisfied, and the remaining 5% expressed feelings of dissatisfaction. The

TABLE 17 MOTHERS' ASSESSMENTS OF INFANTS' HEALTH STATUS FOR THOSE INTERVIEWED TWICE (N = 142)

	Interview I	Interview II
Excellent	60%	39%
Good	30%	41%
Average	9%	17%
Poor	1%	3%

**TABLE 18   INFANTS' HEALTH PROBLEMS
REQUIRING MEDICAL ATTENTION[a]**

	Interview I (N = 184)	Interview II (N = 144)
Ear, nose and throat problems	29%	44%
Bowel-related problems	13%	26%
Skin infections/rashes/allergies	10%	10%
Eating problems	4%	5%
Congenital problems	2%[b]	2%[c]
Accidents	0%	5%[d]
Other	7%[e]	11%[f]

[a] Each percentage is based on the total number of infants. Some infants had more than one problem.

[b] Birth injury (2), orthopedic problem (1), heart murmur (1).

[c] Undeveloped esophagus (1), cranial defect—no fontanel ("soft spot") (1), enlarged liver (1).

[d] Bruises (2), lacerations (2), burns (1), fractured skull (1), poisoning—swallowed paint (1).

[e] Hernia (5), eye infections (4), other minor medical problems (2), measles (1).

[f] Other minor medical problems (6), eye infections (4), anemia (3), meningitis and arthritis (1), recircumcision (1), tumor on neck (1).

reasons for satisfaction most frequently mentioned were quality care and prompt service. Complaints included long waits for care and the unwillingness of medical professionals to answer questions. The older adolescents in Epstein's [1980] sample also voiced criticisms about not receiving adequate answers to their health-related questions.

THE INFANTS' PHYSICAL, COGNITIVE, AND SOCIAL DEVELOPMENT

The Developmental Profile   Alpern and Boll's *Developmental Profile* [1972] was used at the follow-up interview to assess the babies' functioning in five specific areas: physical, self-help, social, academic, and communication. Each respondent was read an inventory of skills arranged in five scales and asked if her infant did or was able to perform the activities specified. The inventory provides an individual profile of the child's developmental functioning by classifying his or her abilities according to age norms (the age at which children usually acquire the skills). Alpern and Boll's descriptions of the five areas for which developmental ages were calculated are the following:

Physical Age	This scale measures the child's physical development by determining his abilities with tasks requiring large and small muscle coordination, strength, stamina, flexibility, and sequential control skills.
Self-Help Age	This scale measures children's abilities to cope independently with the environment and measures the child's skills with such socialization tasks as eating, dressing, and working. This scale evaluates the degree to which children are capable of responsibly caring for themselves and others.
Social Age	This scale measures the child's interpersonal relationship abilities. The child's emotional needs for people, as well as his manner in relating to friends, relatives, and various adults exemplify the skills which measure the child's functioning in the social situation.
Academic Age	This scale measures the child's intellectual abilities by evaluating, at pre-school levels, the development of skills prerequisite to scholastic functioning and, at the school age levels, actual academic achievements.
Communication Age	This scale measures the child's expressive and receptive communication skills with both verbal and non-verbal languages. The child's use and understanding of spoken, written, and gesture languages are evaluated by this scale.

[Alpern and Boll 1972:1]

The *Developmental Profile* [Alpern and Boll 1972] was originally standardized on a population of both black and white children from large, midwestern urban areas who were full-term at birth, not hospitalized during the first 2 weeks of life, and free of any handicapping conditions. No significant differences in development by the sex, race, and socioeconomic status of the children were found in the standarization study.

Once the *Developmental Profile* [Alpern and Boll 1972] had been scored and the five developmental ages calculated for each infant, the difference in months between the child's developmental age and his or her chronological age was computed. Table 19 on page 56 displays the distribution of the five difference scores.

As table 19 indicates, most of the babies had skills that were several months advanced for their ages in all developmental areas. They appear particularly advanced in their social and self-help abilities. The five difference scores were highly intercorrelated (average r = .53; individual correlations ranged from .42 to .63), so one can infer that if a child is advanced in one developmental area, he or she is likely to be advanced in the others. Seventy-two percent of the sample had developmental ages in all five

TABLE 19 ALPERN & BOLL'S DEVELOPMENTAL PROFILE—DISTRIBUTION OF DIFFERENCES BETWEEN INFANT'S FIVE DEVELOPMENTAL AGES AND CHRONOLOGICAL AGE (CA) (N = 142)

Relationship of Developmental Age to Chronological Age	Developmental Areas				
	Physical	Self-help	Social	Academic	Communication
BELOW CA					
5 months or more below	1%	3%	1%	2%	5%
2 to 4 months below	15%	7%	2%	7%	13%
AT CA					
1 month below to 1 month above	20%	9%	6%	24%	15%
ABOVE CA					
2 to 4 months above	23%	18%	16%	30%	26%
5 to 7 months above	16%	11%	19%	20%	23%
8 to 10 months above	15%	20%	26%	8%	11%
11 months or more above	10%	32%	30%	9%	7%
Range	6 mos. below to 21 mos. above CA	7 mos. below to 28 mos. above CA	7 mos. below to 29 mos. above CA	11 mos. below to 19 mos. above CA	7 mos. below to 25 mos. above CA
Mean number of months developmental age exceeds CA	4.0 mos.	7.9 mos.	8.0 mos.	3.8 mos.	3.5 mos.
Standard Deviation	5.3 mos.	7.2 mos.	5.6 mos.	4.8 mos.	3.5 mos.

areas that were at or above age level. The other 28% had skills assessed as being below age level in at least one developmental area. Just 7% of the babies had scores below age level in three or more areas.

None of the five *Developmental Profile* [Alpern and Boll 1972] difference scores was significantly correlated with prematurity or low birth weight, factors often predisposing infants to delays in development. The negative effects of being born too soon or too small had probably all but disappeared by the time of the second interview, when the babies were approximately 18 months old. The difference scores also did not vary significantly by any of the following variables pertaining to the baby's learning environment: whether the child was cared for by someone other than his or her mother or the number of hours per day of such care, who the alternative caretaker was, whether there were other children aged 6 or younger residing in the home, or with whom the baby and mother lived. As mentioned previously, the mother's knowledge of appropriate child development expectations, as evidenced on the *Knowledge Scale* [Epstein 1980], was not a strong predictor of the baby's advanced ability either, nor was her past attendance at special school programs during pregnancy or the first few months after delivery, where she probably would have learned about child development and child care. The differences that existed between the children's developmental ages and their chronological ages were also not associated meaningfully with race, the baby's health problems, or past hospitalizations.

It seems that all but a small proportion of the children fared quite well overall during the first 2 years of life. However, one must remember that the *Developmental Profile* [Alpern and Boll 1972] depended entirely on the mothers' reports. Some respondents may have overestimated the child's abilities to impress the interviewer. Although in situations where the interviewer doubted the answers she was instructed to see if the baby actually had the skill or could perform the activity (if the child was present), this was rarely done. However, many of the mothers whose babies were there at the interview had the child demonstrate his or her skills to the interviewer. It was evident that many respondents were proud of their children's accomplishments, perhaps seeing the child's behavior as a reflection of competence as a parent.

One explanation for the children's precocious self-help and social abilities that others, including Furstenberg [1976] and Stevens [1980], have also proposed is that many of the children spend time with other mature adults, mainly their grandmothers, who may provide an environment particularly conducive to the development of early skills. These caretakers may be more verbal, interacting, and nurturant toward the child, since, unlike the young mothers, they probably have fewer competing needs of their own.

Broman [1981] also found the infants of adolescent mothers slightly but still significantly more advanced in mental and motor abilities at 8 months than children born to women aged 20 to 29, when assessed on the *Bayley Scales of Infant Development* [Bayley 1969]. This relationship held for all racial and socioeconomic groups studied. In addition, the babies of younger mothers had higher scores on the scales rating speed of response, activity level, and acceptance of examiner. By the time they were 4 years old, however, the children born to adolescents in the Broman sample no longer had superior abilities but, in fact, had lower IQ scores, less advanced motor development, and a higher frequency of deviant behavior than the children of older mothers. At age 7, these children still had lower IQ scores and were more frequently rated as deviant in behavior. They were also more often below average in their academic achievement. Broman [1981] suggests that the effects of environmental deficits related to early childbearing appear first in the preschool and early school-age periods, and stresses that the effects of socioeconomic status are even more important at this time than maternal age.

Baldwin and Cain [1980] have extensively reviewed studies focusing on the development of children born to teenagers. They write, "All analyses show deficits in the cognitive development of children (especially male children) born to teenagers; much, but not all, of the effect results from the social and economic consequences of early childbearing" [Baldwin and Cain 1980:34].

Furstenberg [1976] has also found in his Baltimore-based study that children of primarily low-income black adolescent mothers had lower scores on an assessment of school preparedness [*Preschool Inventory* (Educational Testing Service 1970)] at 42 to 60 months than children whose mothers delayed initial childbearing until they were older. However, he did not find a significant relationship between maternal age and the child's cognitive development within his sample of adolescent mothers. Children whose mothers were under 16 when they were born fared as well as those whose mothers were 16 to 18 years old at delivery. The amount of time the mother spent with her child was inversely related to the child's cognitive abilities, as measured by the *Preschool Inventory* [Educational Testing Service 1970]. Children of mothers who attended school or held a job scored higher than those whose mothers stayed home. Furstenberg suggests that the child may benefit from having a more mature, experienced caretaker, often the child's grandmother or other close relative, when his or her mother is away. In addition, one must remember that the mothers who were working or in school were generally more economically advantaged than those who stayed at home, and that the socioeconomic status of the mother was strongly associated with the cognitive test scores of her child.

According to Baldwin and Cain's [1980] review, the relationship between maternal age and the child's social and emotional development is less clear. Furstenberg [1976] found no major differences in this area between children aged 42 to 60 months born to adolescents and those born to older women.

However, he determined that children from economically advantaged families (both one and two parents) scored higher on efficacy and trust measures. Marecek [1979] determined that maternal age had little impact on the child's social and emotional development at age 4 but did significantly affect it at age 7, with children born to black, urban mothers under 18 being more likely to be overactive, hostile, and lacking impulse control.

The discrepancies between the findings regarding the development of children born to adolescent mothers may be attributable to several factors, the first being the age of the children studied. The younger the children, the better they seem to be faring. In this study of babies about 18 months old and Broman's study of 8-month-old infants, the children had abilities at or above age level. Other researchers have determined that by age 4, children of teenagers were behind their peers in cognitive development. It may be that young mothers can cope with the needs infants have for stimulation but not those of preschool-aged children. They may not be able to create and sustain environments that encourage learning or promote the acquisition of skills for older children. The infants' development may also be enhanced by other nurturant caretakers, in this study most often the maternal grandmother. Alternate caretakers such as grandmothers or aunts may be unable or unwilling to care for the toddler or preschool youngster, or may have a different impact upon him or her if they do. These findings have major implications for those involved in educational programs for very young children, particularly in terms of the timing and continuity of such programs.

Another explanation for the apparent differences in the findings regarding the children's abilities is the type of measures used to assess development. Few good measures of cognitive performance or social maturity in very young children currently exist. The multidimensional quality of Alpern and Boll's [1972] *Developmental Profile*, used in this study of young adolescent mothers, may, in part, explain the advanced abilities of the babies at 18 months. While other researchers have relied solely on indicators of cognitive development, this study investigated the child's physical, self-help, social, and communication abilities as well, a better overall indication of the child's performance in the opinion of this researcher. The Alpern and Boll measure also depended on the mothers' reports derived from their day-to-day experience with the baby, while the instruments used by most other researchers required the child's actual performance in a one-time, test situation. It should also be noted that others who have used the *Developmental Profile* [Alpern and Boll 1972] with preschool children enrolled in Head Start programs [Development Associates 1981] have found above-age average scores in all areas. As in our study, self-help and social abilities were the most advanced.

Mothers' Assessments More than half of the respondents (55%) who participated in the second interview said the baby had skills that were "just

TABLE 20   FREQUENT PROBLEMS WITH THE CHILDREN—INTERVIEW II (N = 144)

Behaving the way you want	64%
Controlling his/her temper	45%
Stopping crying when you leave	43%
Quieting down when you're not in the mood for playing	37%
Sleeping at night	34%
Eating at mealtimes	34%

about right" for the child's age level. Forty-one percent thought that the infant was advanced, and the remaining 4% assessed the child as being a bit delayed in development. The respondents' assessments of the child's abilities did not vary according to the number of hours each day the child was cared for by others or their appraisal of how easy things were now with the baby. The mothers' assessments of whether the child was advanced were not highly correlated with the scores on Alpern and Boll's [1972] *Developmental Profile*. However, respondents who said they had read extensively about parenting and child care and those who had a more accurate knowledge of child development, as evidenced on the *Knowledge Scale* [Epstein 1980] (see chapter 5), were more likely to say the baby was advanced (although differences were not significant at the .05 level). This group may be more familiar with the developmental process and thus better observers of the child's acquisition of new skills and somewhat precocious abilities. It should also be noted that white mothers were far more likely than black mothers to view the baby as advanced.

Problems with the Babies   During the second interview, the respondents seen again were asked if they *often* had any of six specific problems with the child, such as getting the baby to sleep at night or to behave in the way they wanted. The incidence of these different problems is shown in table 20.

The number of problems ranged from 0 to 6; the mean was 2.5. Only 8% indicated that they did not often have difficulties such as these with the child. The number of frequently occurring problems did not vary significantly according to the baby's age, race, or the number of hours each day he or she was cared for by someone other than the mother, or who the alternate caretaker was.

Half of the sample (51%) thought it was worth consulting a professional such as a doctor, teacher, or social worker when they had problems such as these with the child. The others said they would seek advice from relatives or rely on their own judgment. The respondent's willingness to turn to a professional did not differ by her current living arrangement, school status, or past use of a special school program either before or after delivery.

MAKING IMPORTANT DECISIONS REGARDING THE BABIES

During both interviews, the respondents were asked who would make important decisions regarding the baby (i.e., special medical care or schools). Their answers are displayed in table 21. More than half of the respondents who were interviewed twice reported at both sessions that they would decide these issues in conjunction with their mothers. Sizable proportions at each time said they would make these decisions alone or in consultation with the babies' fathers. The differences between the respondents' answers to this question at the two interviews were not statistically significant.

As might be expected, at both interview times more of the respondents who were living with their mothers said that they would include them in making decisions. A significant relationship also existed between the infant's sex and who would be involved. Those respondents with a daughter were more likely to say they would resolve these issues themselves or else consult with their mothers only, whereas those with a son were more likely to turn to the baby's father or someone else other than or in addition to their mothers.

Zitner and Miller [1980] found that similar proportions of the slightly older teenage mothers they interviewed about a year and a half after delivery said they would rely on their mothers or the baby's father in making decisions concerning the child and themselves. Fifty-eight percent of that sample reported that they would turn to their mothers for advice. Seventeen percent of the total group indicated they would consult with the baby's father

TABLE 21   WHO WOULD MAKE IMPORTANT DECISIONS REGARDING THE BABIES—THOSE RESPONDENTS INTERVIEWED TWICE (N = 139)

	At Interview I	At Interview II
Respondent alone	16%	22%
Respondent with own mother only	50%	45%
Respondent with baby's father only	18%	8%
Respondent with own mother and baby's father	6%	4%
Respondent with other relative	2%	5%
Respondent's mother alone	4%	12%
Other (baby's father alone, maternal relative alone, or foster parent alone)	4%	4%

or a male partner, and 14% with other relatives. In all, nearly 20% reported that they would not seek out others.

CHAPTER SUMMARY

The average infant was about 3½ months old at the first interview, and 18 months old at the second. The baby's mother assessed his or her health status as "excellent" at the initial interview but had downgraded her appraisal to "good" by the time of the follow-up. This is not surprising in light of the fact that the child had experienced frequent colds and bowel and other health problems necessitating medical attention during the interval between the two sessions. The baby had between four and six checkups by the time he or she was about 18 months old, but continued to have recurring respiratory illnesses and other problems, a finding that is cause for concern. The mother was satisfied with the health care her infant had received but complained that at times medical professionals did not fully answer her questions.

According to the mother's report at the second interview, the typical baby had skills that were, on the average, 5 months advanced for his or her current age. The baby appeared particularly precocious in self-help and social abilities. The child's development may be enhanced by the presence of another more mature caretaker, in most cases the grandmother, who can provide an enriched, supportive learning environment. Other researchers have also found that infants of teenage mothers fare as well during the first 2 years of life as those born to women who are 20 or older. However, most concur that deficits become evident during the later preschool years in children born to very young parents, particularly in cognitive abilities. They attribute these differences to poor learning environments, often resulting from the lower socioeconomic status and truncated education of a mother who began childbearing in adolescence. The need to follow these children through the first few years of life until they enter public school is clear. Suggestions for possible intervention strategies in view of these findings are presented in chapter 12.

CHAPTER SEVEN

The Babies' Fathers

CHARACTERISTICS OF THE BABIES' FATHERS

Age The babies' fathers' ages at the time of the first interview ranged from 14 to 35 years; the median was 17.7. Forty-three percent of the fathers were younger than 18; 45% were between 18 and 20; and most of the others were in their early 20s. These findings are comparable to those of Zelnik and Kantner's [1980] previous surveys of 15- to 19-year-old women, whose sexual partners were most likely to have been about 2 years older.

Incest and Rape During the first interview, the mothers were asked if they were related to the baby's father in any way. All responded negatively. As mentioned previously, the pregnancies of four of the respondents allegedly resulted from rape.

Marital Status Most of the fathers had never been married (92%). Only two were married at the first interview, both to respondents, but seven had been married before that time. The marital status of six fathers was unknown.

School Status The fathers' school status as reported by the respondents seen at the two interview times is displayed in table 22 on page 64. Fewer fathers were known to be attending school at the follow-up session.

Interestingly enough, there was a significant positive relationship between the father's school status and the mother's school status; if the mother was in school, the father was more likely to be enrolled.

Employment Status More than half of the fathers were employed when the first interview was conducted (59%). Another 8% were not in contact with the baby's mother and their employment status was unknown. The other

TABLE 22   BABIES' FATHERS' SCHOOL STATUS

	At Interview I (N = 184)	At Interview II (N = 144)
Attending school	40%[a]	31%[b]
Not attending school		
Graduated from high school	21%	23%
Dropped out before graduation	28%	26%
Dropped out but last grade completed unknown	6%	11%
School status unknown	5%	9%

[a] Includes 13 fathers who had graduated from high school.

[b] Includes 10 fathers who had graduated from high school.

33% were not working at this time. Most of the fathers who were employed had service (15%), labor (9%), or skilled, operative (10%) positions, according to the mothers, but a sizable proportion of the mothers could not describe the father's employment (23%). By the time of the second interview, the proportion of respondents seen again who knew the baby's father was employed had decreased from 59% to 35%. The group of fathers known to be not working had increased from 32% to 41%, and those whose employment status was unknown, from 9% to 24%. If only those fathers whose employment status was known are considered, 64% were working at the time of the first interview compared to 46% at the follow-up session.

Acknowledgment of Paternity   Eighty-seven percent of the respondents said during the initial interview that the baby's father acknowledged paternity. Another 8% said that the father did not, and the remaining 5% were unsure.

Counseling   Less than a fifth of the fathers had received counseling either before or after the birth of the baby, 6% before and 12% after. For most, the content of the counseling focused on decisions about keeping the infant, legal responsibilities of paternity, and birth control methods.

CONTACT BEFORE PREGNANCY

Almost three-quarters of the respondents seen for the first interview had known the father for a year or more before they became pregnant (73%). An additional 21% had been acquainted with him for between 3 to 11 months. The other 6% had known the father for periods of less than 3 months, including four mothers who said they had only seen the baby's father once. More of the black respondents than white respondents had known the baby's father for a year or longer. Fathers who were younger than 18 were also more likely to have been in contact for longer periods than were those who were older.

Williams [1977], as well as other researchers, also found that the adolescents he studied had lengthy relationships with the baby's father before becoming pregnant; 80% had dated him for a year or longer. The notion of a short, sporadic relationship between the teenager and her baby's father does not appear to be supported.

CONTACT DURING PREGNANCY AND AT BOTH INTERVIEW TIMES

Table 23 displays the frequency of the respondents' contacts with the baby's father during pregnancy and at both interview times for the group of young mothers who were seen twice. Most of these respondents saw the father frequently during pregnancy; in fact, 60% visited with him every day. By the time of the first interview, the frequency of contacts for more than half (53%) had decreased. However, 35% continued to see the father as often as they had during pregnancy, and contact for the other 12% had increased during this period. Twenty-five percent no longer were in touch with the father, a proportion comparable to that in Furstenberg's [1976] sample of slightly older mothers one year after delivery.

Frequency of contact between the respondent and the father at the first interview was significantly related to the amount of contact they had during pregnancy, with more of those who had many visits in the past continuing to see each other regularly. Thus black respondents were far more likely than white respondents to be seeing the father then. Contact at this time was not associated in any meaningful way with the length of time the father had been known prior to pregnancy, his age or school status, or the mother's living arrangement at the time.

By the follow-up interview, the proportion of respondents who were still in contact with the baby's father had diminished from 75% to 65%. The frequency of contact for 39% of the mothers who still saw the father had decreased substantially from the time of the initial interview. However, 37%

TABLE 23 FREQUENCY OF CONTACT BETWEEN THE RESPONDENT AND THE BABY'S FATHER FOR THOSE RESPONDENTS INTERVIEWED TWICE

	During Pregnancy	At Interview I	At Interview II
Every day	60%	35%	22%
Several times a week	27%	22%	17%
Once a week	6%	7%	6%
Once a month	2%	4%	10%
Less than once a month	5%	7%	10%
Not at all	0%	25%	35%

were with the baby's father as often as they had been, and contact had increased for the other 24%. The study mothers are similar to older adolescents in the relationships they had with the baby's father. Zitner and Miller [1980] determined that 62% of the slightly older teenage mothers they studied were still in touch with the father about 17 months postpartum. The substantial decline over time in contact between teenage mothers and the baby's father has also been found in other studies [Furstenberg 1976, Williams 1977].

The mother's contact with the father at the second interview was again significantly related to how long the two had known each other before she became pregnant, and how often they had visited during the pregnancy, as well as to the frequency of their meetings in the first few months after delivery. Those who had been acquainted for longer periods and those who had seen each other frequently in the past were more likely to still be in contact at 18 months postpartum. As might be expected, the fathers who acknowledged paternity were also more likely to be seen by the mothers at this time.

Contact with the baby's father at the follow-up session was not significantly associated with the mothers' age; school status; living arrangement then; or the experience of a subsequent pregnancy; or her aspirations regarding marriage, children, or education. Neither was it related to the baby's age or sex, or the father's age, school, or employment status.

CONTACTS BETWEEN THE FATHERS AND THE BABIES

Sixty-five percent of the infants had some regular contact with their fathers at the time of the first interview, several months after delivery. As would be expected, this was highly dependent on the mother's relationship with the father at the time. Of those babies whose mothers did not see the father, only a few were visited by their fathers. Black male infants were far more likely than white male infants to spend time with their fathers. There were no significant racial differences in fathers' visiting of daughters.

By the second interview, the proportion of babies seeing their fathers had decreased from 67% to 55%. Twelve percent of all the children whose mothers were interviewed again saw their fathers every day, 17% several times a week, 7% once a week, and the other 19% less frequently. Most of the babies who were no longer in contact with their fathers had a mother who had also stopped seeing the father during the interval between the two interviews. Frequency of contact at this time was not related in any meaningful way to the mothers' and babies' current living arrangements. Forty-eight percent of the mothers interviewed thought the baby's father spent the right amount of time with the child; another 48% believed the time was inadequate; and the other 4% said it was too much.

Help from the Babies' Fathers The respondents were questioned during the initial interview about the help they received from the baby's father. Two out of five said that the father contributed to the family's income (41%). The extent of this financial support was not determined. A similar proportion of the mothers reported that the father gave them clothes or other material items such as diapers or food (44%), and 14 said that he helped with medical expenses. In all, 59% of the fathers provided some type of support. According to the respondents, the other 41% had given them nothing in the form of concrete help.

Assistance from the babies' fathers during pregnancy and the first few months after delivery was significantly related to the frequency of the father's contact with the mother then, and how long they had known each other. Respondents who saw the baby's father frequently and those who had known him for 6 months or longer before becoming pregnant were more likely to be receiving help. Help from the fathers did not vary according to their ages or employment status at the time.

For those respondents interviewed twice, financial and material support from the father had decreased substantially by the time of the second interview. The proportion who said the father contributed to the family income had dropped from 40% to 25%. Much of the reduction in support is attributable to the decrease in the proportion of respondents still in contact with the father 18 months after delivery. At this time, more of the black mothers received monetary support from the father than the white mothers did. The younger respondents were also more likely to be getting money at this time from the father than the older ones, 46% of the 14- and 15-year-olds versus 18% of the 16-year-olds and 22% of those 17. It is also worth mentioning that the young teenage mothers in this study were far less likely to be helped financially by the father a year and a half after delivery than were the older adolescent mothers in Zitner and Miller's [1980] sample.

Almost all of the sample indicated at the follow-up session that the father gave them small amounts of money or gifts, as well as diapers and food, but for most this was an infrequent occurrence, usually less than once a month. Only a fourth of the fathers helped care for the child as often as once a week (28%). A similar proportion were involved in decision making regarding the baby (25%).

Half of the respondents seen for a second interview said that the baby's father had provided them with less help than they had expected before the delivery (49%). Nearly a third (31%) said they had received about as much assistance as they had anticipated, and the others had been helped more by the father than they thought they would be. It is clear that most had unrealistic expectations about the support the father either could or would provide.

CHAPTER SUMMARY

At the first interview, the average baby's father was almost 18 years old, not attending school, and employed in a service-related job. He had not finished high school or passed an equivalency examination at this time.

The typical father had known his baby's mother for a year or longer before she became pregnant, and they had seen each other several times each week throughout the pregnancy. A year and a half after the delivery, the baby's father still saw the mother and baby, but less often. The father provided disposable diapers and small amounts of money, but not consistently or frequently. The extent of support he provided was not what the mother had anticipated before the baby's birth.

The question of the baby's father's role is important. Few fathers received any services during pregnancy or immediately after delivery to help them make well-informed decisions or cope effectively as a parent. This is a concern, since many do influence considerably the mothers' decisions during the pregnancy, and later they frequently care for the children. Even though by law, in most localities, teenage fathers have rights and privileges, few professionals view them as an integral part of the picture. Those who do have found it extremely difficult to engage the fathers in program activities. Much progress has been made, however, in recent years by using such approaches as male counselors in schools and social service agencies, and storefront locations for family planning clinics.

The professional dilemma remains as to how much to encourage the relationship between the teenage mother and her baby's father. Clearly, they both share responsibilities toward the child. Promoting their staying together, however, may result in a too-early (teenage) marriage, with probable subsequent economic difficulty and perhaps a family size larger than desirable.

CHAPTER EIGHT

The Mothers' Parents

CHARACTERISTICS OF THE PARENTS

Age Eighty-seven percent of the respondents knew the ages of their mothers or stepmothers, if the parent or stepparent was living at the first interview. Ages ranged from 21 to 64 years; the median was 36.7. In contrast, only 37% could say how old their fathers or stepfathers were. The fathers' age range was 25 to 75 years; the median was 40. Most of those who were unfamiliar with their fathers' ages had not been in contact with them in the last few years.

Age at First Birth The 165 respondents' mothers for whom information was available were 11 to 28 years old at the time of their first live births. Mean age then was 17.4 years. One-quarter had first delivered at age 15 or younger, and another 57% between the ages of 16 and 19. The other 18% had given birth to a first child when they were 20 or older.

Other researchers have also found a high incidence of repetition of adolescent pregnancy from generation to generation. In Furstenberg's [1976] study of predominantly black lower and working class teenage mothers who were on the average slightly older than the mothers in this study, nearly half of the grandmothers had delivered a first child when they were younger than 18.

Forty-one percent of the sample respondents had sisters who had been pregnant when adolescent. Most of the sisters had carried to term and kept the baby. Having a sister who had previously been pregnant as a teenager did not seem to influence significantly the respondent's initial reaction to pregnancy, the timing or amount of prenatal care she obtained, her appropriate knowledge of child development expectations, or use of or familiarity with contraceptives.

Marital Status At the time of the first interview, one-third of the respondents' mothers were married, 22% to the respondents' fathers and 11% to other men. Half were separated (28%) or divorced (23%). Another 6% were widowed, and the remaining 10% had never been married. Significant racial differences existed in the marital status of the respondents' mothers, with more of the whites than blacks having mothers who were currently married. The percentage of single-parent households in this study population is more than three times larger than that found nationwide in 1979 among families with children under 18 [U.S. Bureau of the Census 1980a]. Others, including Furstenberg [1976] and Epstein [1980], have also determined that a high proportion of the teenagers they studied came from one-parent families.

Education Just 35% of all the respondents' fathers and 45% of all their mothers were known to have completed high school. However, some others had received specialized training related to their employment. In all, 28% of the mothers and 12% of the fathers had attended vocational programs, the mothers most frequently to develop skills in nursing, cosmetology, or business; the fathers for training in auto mechanics, construction, or management.

Employment Status According to the Respondents Sixty-three percent of the respondents' fathers and 40% of their mothers were employed at the time of the first interview. Most of the fathers worked in construction or in factories in skilled or semiskilled jobs; the mothers in clerical or service-related positions such as waitresses or maids. Mothers who had completed more years of formal education were more likely to be employed than those who had not. It must be noted that the mothers' current employment status was not significantly influenced by the presence of a child younger than 7 in the home in addition to the respondent's infant. And only a few mothers said that they had left their jobs in the last year because they had to care for their daughters' babies.

NUMBER OF PERSONS IN THE HOUSEHOLD

The number of persons residing in the respondents' households at the initial interview ranged from 3 to 15, including the respondent and her infant. The mean was 6.7, a figure substantially higher than the national average of 2.75 for households with children under 18 [U.S. Bureau of the Census 1980b]. Nearly a third of the households included one or more children younger than 7 years in addition to the respondents' babies.

PROBLEMS WITH HOUSING

During the first interview, the mothers were asked about 11 different problems their families might be having with housing. The number of current problems ranged from 0 to 8; the mean for the total sample was 1.7. Thirty-seven percent reported no problems. As table 24 indicates, problems with safety, apartment or house size, rodents, or waits for repairs were more prevalent than difficulty with utilities. The number of housing problems was significantly related to the respondent's receipt of public assistance, with more of those receiving support listing a large number of problems. It also tended, although the differences were not statistically significant at the .05 level, to be associated with relative socioeconomic status; those whose family's status was lower mentioned more problems. No significant racial differences were apparent in the number of housing problems.

Concern over the security of the apartment or house against break-ins was highly correlated with a variety of the other housing problems, and is therefore a strong predictor of overall housing inadequacy for this population. In addition, utility problems relating to heat, hot water, electricity, and the telephone were significantly intercorrelated. Although the incidence of any of these individual problems is relatively low, the few families reporting one such difficulty tend to have multiple problems.

FAMILY INCOME

The sources of income for the families of the respondents seen for both interviews are summarized in table 25 on page 72.

Parents' employment as a source of family income remained essentially the same from the first interview to the second despite a slight decrease during that period in the percentage of respondents living with either one or both parents. It is worth noting that the proportion of the sample supported by their parents more than a year after delivery was not significantly

TABLE 24   HOUSING PROBLEMS LISTED AT INTERVIEW I (N = 184)

HEALTH AND SAFETY	
Neighborhood unsafe	39%
Rats and mice	27%
Apartment/house too small	26%
Repairs not made soon enough	26%
Apartment/house not safe against break-ins	24%
UTILITIES	
No working telephone	9%
No heat	8%
No hot water	5%
Stove not working	4%
No electricity	2%
Refrigerator not working	2%

TABLE 25 SOURCES OF FAMILY INCOME FOR THOSE RESPONDENTS INTERVIEWED TWICE. PERCENTAGE OF FAMILIES (N = 144)

	At Interview I	At Interview II
EMPLOYMENT		
Parents' employment	53%	57%
Respondent's employment	9%	15%
INFORMAL SUPPORTS		
Other relatives	21%	14%
Baby's father	40%	25%
PUBLIC SUPPORT		
Public Assistance (predominently AFDC)	60%	85%
Food stamps	24%	52%
WIC (Women, Infants and Children food supplement program)	48%	38%
Other (Parents' Social Security, Unemployment Compensation, or Veterans' Compensation or Other)	22%	25%

different from what Zitner and Miller [1980] found among older teenagers. Assistance from other informal sources such as relatives had declined substantially, however, between the two interviews, but these differences were not statistically significant at the .05 level. No racial differences were apparent at either interview in the support provided to the respondents by their parents or other relatives. Financial assistance from the baby's father and the diminution in that help over time were discussed in chapter 7.

While the extent of the support provided to the sample respondents by their parents stayed about the same between the two interviews, and that given by other relatives and the baby's father diminished, dependence on public sources of financial assistance, such as Aid to Families with Dependent Children (AFDC) and food stamps, increased significantly. The use of WIC, a supplemental food program for pregnant women and parents of young children, had also declined by the second interview (18 months postpartum) but this decrease is due, in part, to time limitations on eligibility at the study locations.

Almost all the respondents who obtained public assistance at the first interview said they received AFDC (93%). The other 7% received general assistance. More than half of the respondents got the AFDC check in their own names (54%), but payments for 40% were sent to their mothers and for 6% to relatives or guardians. Significantly more of the older respondents got the checks in their own names.

Use of public assistance at the time of the first interview was significantly related to the following: the marital status of the respondent's parents, the number of housing problems her family experienced, and use of food stamps. As would be expected, respondents whose mothers were no longer married to their fathers were more likely to be getting public assistance than those whose parents were still married. Thus, more of those living with their mothers only were receiving support. Use of public assistance was also strongly correlated with a large number of housing problems and receipt of food stamps. This last finding is consistent with the national figures issued in 1979 by the Social Security Administration [U.S. DHEW 1979] showing that three out of four AFDC families also received food stamps.

Use of the various types of public assistance—AFDC, food stamps, and WIC—at the time of the follow-up interview did not differ significantly by the respondent's living arrangement then or whether she had changed her living arrangement since the initial interview. Neither were there strong racial differences in the receipt of these services at this time or at the first interview.

It is worth adding that the proportion of the young adolescent mothers in this study who obtained public assistance about a year and a half after delivery (85%) was significantly greater than that found by Zitner and Miller [1980] in their sample of slightly older teenagers (50%). The younger adolescents have no real alternatives for financial support other than their families and welfare, while older teenagers have some, although slight, chances for employment.

SOCIOECONOMIC STATUS

The socioeconomic characteristics of the respondents' parents were used instead of their own in the development of a status measure, in view of the ages of the mothers and their dependence on their families for financial support. Almost all of the respondents ranked in the lower socioeconomic categories in Hollingshead's [1957] index of status positions ranked by the occupation and educational level of the male head of household. To provide some variation within that range, a two-factor version of Green's [1970] three-factor model was used to reflect the relative socioeconomic status of each mother's family. The two variables in this index were the respondent's mother's educational level and the occupation of the main parental wage earner in the respondent's household. In situations where neither parent was currently employed, their usual occupations were used in the index if they had been working any time in the last 2 years. The choice of the mother's educational level over the father's seemed particularly pertinent for this sample since so many of the mothers were living in female-headed families. Green originally selected the mother's educational level because he found it to be more highly correlated than the father's with a composite measure of preventive health behavior.

Using Green's index, sufficient information was available for classifying 89% of the study sample. Scores were provided by Green for coding the number of years of education completed by the female head of household and the occupation of the highest wage earner. These scores were weighted in the following manner and then combined to compute the SES score: (.7 multiplied by education score) + (.4 multiplied by occupation score). The range of possible SES scores was approximately 30 to 85. The range for this sample was 31 to 77; the median was 50.8. Forty-five percent of the respondents had low family SES scores relative to others in the sample (30–48); 50% had mid-range scores (49–67); and the remaining 5% had high scores (68–85). This relative family SES classification was used for cross-sectional analyses of the findings.

CHAPTER SUMMARY

The typical respondent's mother was 37 years old at the time of the first interview; her father was 40 years old. The mean age at first birth for the respondents' mothers was 17.4 years; 82% had delivered a first baby when they were teenagers. The high incidence of generational repetition and the prevalence of early births among the respondents' sisters strongly suggest that the adolescent mother's entire family could benefit from a comprehensive, coordinated service program.

The typical respondent's mother was not married at the time of the first interview. The single-parent female-headed household was by far the most common living arrangement for those in the study sample, much more prevalent than that found nationwide. The average respondent's mother had not completed high school but had attended a special training program related to her job. Both the typical respondent's mother and father were employed at the time of the first interview. The family income was generally supplemented by the AFDC grant the respondent received.

Dependence on AFDC was also the rule for most of the respondent's peers who had become pregnant. Reliance on this source of income increases as the baby grows older and help from family, the baby's father, and friends decreases.

The extensive, long-term public costs of adolescent parenthood have been emphasized by many researchers. In a recent report issued by SRI International [1979], the net present value of governmental expenditures (federal, state, and local) for teenagers giving birth in 1979 for medical and welfare costs alone that will be required over 20 years as a consequence of the early births was estimated to be no less than $8 billion. While these figures on governmental expenditures are certainly staggering, the full economic impact of adolescent parenthood on other members of the family is unknown. The already limited financial resources of the adolescent's family are stretched even further by the event of an early pregnancy. The accommodations and compromises the extended family has to make in terms of reentry into the labor market, child care, additional educational or training opportunities, and housing arrangements are also factors to be taken into consideration.

CHAPTER NINE
Child Care Arrangements

Eighty-seven percent of the respondents interviewed twice had their infants cared for by someone else for at least part of every day at the time of the first interview. This proportion remained about the same at the follow-up interview (89%). However, the amount of care for 40% of the babies had increased during the period between the two interviews. For another 23% it had decreased, and for the other 37% it remained essentially the same. The actual number of hours the babies spent in care daily is summarized in table 26. As the table indicates, two out of three infants were away from their mothers 5 or more hours daily throughout their first 18 months.

The extensive amount of nonmaternal care for the babies in this sample was somewhat greater than what others have found among study populations of adolescent mothers. However, the differences are probably attributable to the younger age of these respondents, their subsequent dependence on their parents, and requirements to attend school. Zitner and Miller [1980] determined that 66% of the slightly older teenagers they interviewed about a year and a half after delivery had child care arrangements for 2 or more hours each day, including 28% whose babies were in care for 8 or more hours daily.

Also, the infants in this study were away from their parents more than most young children. Bane et al., referring to Hayghe's [1978] earlier paper, writes that, "No more than 13% of children from birth to 2 years spent 30 hours a week or more in the care of someone other than a parent" [Bane et al. 1979:54]. Most of the babies in this sample were spending a great deal of time in the care of someone other than their mothers, albeit often their maternal grandmothers. The effect of these care arrangements and multiple mothering situations is as yet not fully known. It must be noted here, however, that despite the fact that two out of three mothers were away from their babies 5 or more hours daily, most said during the follow-up interview that they spent the "right amount of time" with their children (75%). Only 15% thought their time together was "not enough." The other 10% believed they were with their infants "too much."

The respondents whose babies were in care for 5 or more hours daily at both interview times were far more likely to be attending school than those who did not have extensive care arrangements. Thus, they tended to be younger, since more of the older mothers had dropped out of school. At the second interview, 80% of the infants whose mothers were then 14 and 15 years old and 83% of those whose mothers were 16 were cared for by others 5 or more hours daily, versus 62% of those whose mothers were 17. More of the black babies than white babies were also cared for by others for lengthy periods each day at the time of the follow-up interview, but again some of this difference is attributable to the mother's school status as more white than black respondents had stopped attending school at 18 months postpartum.

In addition, significant site differences existed in the amount of child care used at both interviews. More of the respondents in Chicago than in Cleveland or Minneapolis/St. Paul had their babies cared for 5 or more hours daily (at Interview I, 72% in Chicago vs 47% in Minneapolis/St. Paul and 45% in Cleveland). By the time of the follow-up interview, the proportion of respondents whose babies were in care 5 or more hours each day had increased slightly in Chicago and Cleveland to 78% and 52%, respectively, but decreased in Minneapolis/St. Paul to 18%.

The number of hours an infant was cared for by someone other than his or her mother did not vary significantly at either interview by any of the following: who the child's caretaker was, the mother's or baby's age or living arrangement, or the presence of another child in the home younger than 7. At the follow-up session, the extent of child care was also not found to differ by whether the mother had experienced a subsequent pregnancy.

CHILD CARE PROVIDERS
At both interview times, the respondents' mothers were the predominant alternate child care providers in more than half of the families, as table 27 indicates. For the others, respondents' sisters, other relatives, paid babysit-

TABLE 26 AMOUNT OF CHILD CARE USED DAILY FOR THOSE RESPONDENTS INTERVIEWED TWICE (N = 137)

	Interview I	Interview II
None	13%	11%
1 to 4 hours	23%	14%
5 to 8 hours	44%	46%
9 or more hours	20%	29%

TABLE 27 PREDOMINANT CHILD CARE PROVIDERS FOR THOSE RESPONDENTS INTERVIEWED TWICE (N = 144)

	At Interview I	At Interview II
Respondent's mother	53%	62%
Respondent's sister	9%	7%
Other maternal relatives	8%	10%
Paid babysitter	8%	5%
Baby's father and/or family	2%	2%
Day care	4%	1%
Other	3%	2%
No child care	13%	11%

ters, the baby's father and his family, friends, and day care facilities were the sources of child care. It is noteworthy, also, that in 52% of the families where the baby's grandmother provided care, other relatives also supplied short-term babysitting. Many respondents had three or more regular adult caretakers for the infant.

As table 27 shows, the respondents' reliance on their own mothers for child care actually increased from the first to the second interview 18 months after delivery. These young teenagers' dependence on their mothers is much greater than that found among older adolescents. In Zitner and Miller's [1980] study in which the respondents were on the average 16.6 years old at delivery, just 28% had their children cared for by their mothers 2 or more hours daily a year and a half after delivery.

Forty-six percent of the study respondents who were interviewed twice had the same child care arrangements at both times, most often their own mothers. In nearly 4 out of 10 families, the baby had been cared for by the grandmother on a regular basis throughout the first 18 months (39%). A significant portion of the sample, however, had changed the child care provider from the first to the second interview (57%); the largest group (24%) being those who had not been relying on their mothers several months after delivery for child care but were by the time of the follow-up interview. This includes 14 respondents (10%) who had reported at the first session that they had no care arrangements. Eleven percent of the sample whose mothers had been caring for the infant at the first session no longer had them as providers at the second. Many of these respondents had turned to other maternal relatives for babysitting, but a third no longer had anyone else caring for their babies. Most of the other changes in child care arrangements occurred among nonfamilial types of care (baby's father and his family, friends, babysitters, day care, and others).

As might be expected, the child care provider differed significantly by the respondents' living arrangements at both interview times, with those living with their mothers being more likely to have them as the baby's caretaker. Respondents whose mothers were currently employed were less likely to receive regular child care help from them and depended more on nonfamilial sources such as babysitters, friends, and day care. The child care provider did not vary in any meaningful way at either interview by the respondent's age, race, or school status, or the age of her baby. Neither was it influenced significantly by the presence of a child younger than 7 in the household in addition to the respondent's baby, or whether the respondent had become pregnant again, delivered, and kept the infant.

Emergency Child Care   When the respondents were asked during the first interview what they would do in emergency situations if their regular child care arrangement was not available, more than a third answered that other relatives would care for the baby (35%). Another third (32%) said they would stay home themselves or else take the infant with them if they had to go out. Most of the others said they would call on neighbors or friends (14%) or the baby's father's families (12%) for help. At the follow-up interview, the respondents' solutions for emergency child care were similar.

SATISFACTION WITH CHILD CARE ARRANGEMENT

Three-fourths of the respondents interviewed twice who had child care arrangements expressed extreme satisfaction regarding it at both sessions (74% at Interview I, 80% at Interview II). Most of the others said they were satisfied but had some reservations, and a few said they were dissatisfied. The mothers' attitudes did not vary significantly at either interview by who the caretakers were or the infants' ages.

Despite their positive feelings regarding the child care arrangements they had, 45% of the sample reported during the second interview that they had disagreements with caretakers over how things should be done with the baby, and nearly a third said they did not have enough child care. The occurrence of these problems did not differ significantly by who the caretaker was. Since so many of the babies are cared for by their grandmothers, one can only speculate from informal reports that much intergenerational conflict exists regarding such issues as feeding, discipline, and the amount of time the mother spends away from her baby. Service providers should be more attuned to these conflicts and work with the individual family members to resolve them, since it is not economically feasible for the social service system to duplicate in most situations the child care resources the family already offers. Neither is it advisable to allow the strong emotional, social, and financial support network that the extended family provides the teenage mother and her baby to dissolve. This is not to say that out-of-home child care may not be preferable for some babies,

TABLE 28   PREFERENCES FOR ALTERNATE CHILD CARE ARRANGEMENTS AT INTERVIEW I (N = 184)

Would be willing to use:	
relative in young mother's home	73%
relative/close friend in her/his home	69%
child care at school	57%
day care center in neighborhood	47%
babysitter in young mother's home	42%
babysitter in her/his home	39%

particularly where the family's functioning is chaotic or when the conflicts among family members are extreme.

PREFERRED CHILD CARE ALTERNATIVES

In the interest of determining the respondents' attitudes about different child care resources, those who had others caring for their babies on a regular basis at the time of the first interview were asked about their willingness to use different types of child care in the event their current arrangements became unavailable. Table 28 summarizes their preferences.

The respondents' preferences did not differ significantly according to the sex or age of the baby. Neither did they vary by race except as to willingness to use child care at school, about which significantly more of the black than white mothers had positive attitudes. The respondents' opinions reflect their current child care arrangements—choosing help by relatives over other sources. It is significant that school-based child care was selected over other nonfamilial sources, and this finding should be recognized by school officials and community planners, some of whom believe that school-based day care would be unpopular because teenagers do not want to mix their roles as students and parents in the school environment.

CHAPTER SUMMARY

The average respondent had her infant cared for by someone else 5 or more hours daily at both interview times so that she could continue to attend school. Her mother was the baby's predominant alternate child care provider, but other relatives, such as her sister and brother, also babysat for occasional periods. Like her peers, the typical young mother had come to depend more and more on her own mother for child care as her baby grew older and help from others diminished.

The respondents' heavy reliance on their mothers for child care deserves considerable attention. The infants' developmental status may, in fact, be enhanced by these multiple mothering situations, as has been previously discussed in chapter 6. The present study, however, did not attempt to investigate the respondents' mothers' willingness to assume additional child care responsibilities or their attitudes about continuing to care for the baby. Eight of the grandmothers had stopped working to babysit for their daughters' infants. The number prevented or dissuaded from entering the workforce or obtaining additional education or training due to unexpected child care responsibilities is unknown. Certain services such as medical care for the babies and child development information should be directed to the respondents' mothers, as well as to the respondents, since the former provide so much of the daily care for the infant and also act as the prime informational resources for their daughters. However, these women also need help for their own problems, such as how to relate to a daughter who is still a child but also a mother, or their interest in becoming employed and having a role outside of the home. Suggestions for services for this population are discussed further in chapter 12.

CHAPTER TEN

Support Services

USE AND NEED AT THE FIRST INTERVIEW

During the first interview, the respondents were questioned about their use of and need for 16 different support services typically available in urban or suburban communities. Each mother was read a list of services and asked whether she had used any of them since she became pregnant, and whether she currently needed them. The respondents' answers are displayed in table 29. As the table indicates and earlier chapters of this report have shown, medical care for the mother and her baby, parenting or baby care classes, and sex education were the services used by the largest numbers of respondents; 7 out of 10 or more. Counseling and public assistance had also been used by more than half of the sample since they became pregnant.

The number of different services used by the respondents ranged from 0 to 15; the mean was 7. Only one mother indicated that she had not used any of the services listed since she became pregnant. The number of services used was not influenced in any meaningful way by the respondent's age or living arrangement, the socioeconomic status of her family relative to that of others in the sample, or participation in special school programs during pregnancy and/or the immediate postpartum period. However, it was related to receipt of public assistance, with more of those obtaining this type of financial support also receiving many other services. Use of parenting, Lamaze, and sex education classes was also interrelated, with mothers who attended one such type of class being more likely to have been to the others. With the exception of these three kinds of programs and public assistance, however, use of specific services by the young respondents was not highly predictive of the use of other services.

The use of support services by the sample respondents during pregnancy and the first few months after delivery is comparable to what other researchers (e.g., Zitner and Miller 1980) have found among slightly older adolescents at various times both before and after giving birth, with one exception. The youngest teenage mothers appear somewhat more dependent than the older ones on AFDC and other public sources of support, such as food stamps and the WIC program. This is consonant with the fact that their ages almost totally preclude any employment opportunities.

Need for Services The respondents expressed many different needs for support services during the first interview, as table 29 indicates. The number of services needed ranged from 0 to 13; the mean was 3.3. Twenty-one percent of the sample said they did not want any services at this time. It is significant that the number of services needed was not strongly associated with the respondent's family's socioeconomic status relative to that of others in the sample, or whether she was receiving AFDC.

Specific needs for concrete services were the most widespread. Food stamps were the type of assistance most frequently reported as needed at the

TABLE 29 USE OF AND NEED FOR SUPPORT SERVICES AT INTERVIEW I (N = 184)

	Used Since Pregnant	Not Using Now but Need
Medical care for the baby	95%	10%
Medical care for yourself	89%	6%
Sex education—information about preventing pregnancy	74%	12%
Public assistance	60%	30%
Parenting or baby care classes	70%	12%
Counseling	53%	18%
WIC (food supplement program)	48%	31%
Childbirth classes like Lamaze—breathing classes	45%	2%
Babysitters	35%	30%
Food stamps	24%	41%
Counseling about drugs or drinking	23%	7%
Tutoring	13%	24%
Help with legal problems	5%	10%
Day care center	4%	26%
Other (housing, help finding employment)	4%	2%

first interview by 4 out of 10 of the respondents. A third or more said they could use the following services: the WIC program (food supplements), public assistance, material help such as furniture or clothes, babysitters, and recreational activities. Significantly, just 15% listed parenting classes and only 12% named sex education as current needs.

The prevalence of needs for concrete services over other types of help, such as counseling and tutoring, deserves considerable attention. One reason for the lack of interest in the other services may be that the mothers' needs in these areas have already been met by agency services. However, a more likely explanation is that the teenage mothers are more likely to rely on their own families rather than professionals for emotional support, help with decision making, and sources of information about child development and parenting.

Other researchers have also found extensive needs for concrete services among the slightly older teenage mothers they studied a year or more after their first births [Zitner and Miller 1980, Cannon-Bonventre and Kahn 1979]. As might be expected, interest in housing and job training were more prevalent for the older adolescents than for the younger ones. Older teenagers were also more likely to say they needed help with child care at this time. This difference reflects the fact that fewer of the older mothers continued to live with their parents and subsequently did not receive as much help from them.

USE AND NEED AT THE SECOND INTERVIEW

The respondents were also queried in the second interview, approximately 18 months after delivery, about their use of and need for certain services: public assistance, food stamps, baby care classes, and sex education. Their behavior regarding these services has already been described in earlier chapters but will be included here for purposes of comparison.

The proportion of the respondents interviewed twice who were receiving public assistance had increased substantially from the first to the second interview, from 60% to 85%. Consequently, need for this service had diminished from 30% to 6%. The group using food stamps had also grown from 24% at the first interview several months after delivery to 52% at the follow-up session 18 months postpartum. The percentage expressing a need for this type of help had also decreased, from 41% to 26%.

In contrast, fewer respondents attended parenting classes during the interval between the interviews than had before the first session, and the size of the group saying they needed this service had increased from 13% at the first interview to 50% at the second. The proportion of the sample indicating that they wanted sex education also increased between the two interviews from 12% to 24%.

It is clear from these findings that while the need for certain concrete services decreased over time, interest in a variety of others increased. Even 18 months after the birth of a first child, many of the mothers still had financial and informational needs that were not met by their families or by service agencies.

FINANCIAL NEEDS

Other aspects of the mothers' financial needs were also investigated at the follow-up interview. Each respondent was read a list of nine items and asked if there were times when she did not have enough money to pay for any of them. The list and the mothers' answers are displayed in table 30. The number of different financial needs the respondents said they had ranged from 0 to 7; the mean was 2.1. A fifth of the sample reported that they never lacked money for these expenses.

None of the respondents' needs for money at the time of the second interview varied significantly by their ages or living arrangements. One need, however, having money "to go out with friends," did differ by the infants' ages, with more of the respondents with older babies indicating that this was a problem. It may be that as the child grows older, the mothers experience more competition for their limited resources. Since other family members typically cover the costs of the rent and food, the respondents may first identify financial restrictions on their own entertainment and personal expenses as problems.

In addition to these questions about money, the mothers were asked what they did when financial problems occurred. The most frequently mentioned answer given by 35% of the respondents who had financial problems was to obtain help from parents. A similar proportion of the sample said they would do without the item or service they needed or wait until they had money for

TABLE 30   PERCENTAGE OF RESPONDENTS REPORTING OCCASIONAL LACK OF MONEY AT INTERVIEW II (N = 144)

For their clothes or other things they need (e.g., cosmetics, magazines, school or training program fees)	58%
To go out with friends	44%
For the baby's clothes or diapers	34%
For the baby's food	33%
For babysitters or day care	19%
For bills (e.g., utilities, phone, household repairs)	14%
For medicine	6%
To go to the doctor or to take the baby to the doctor	5%
For rent	3%

it (33%). Sixteen percent said they would rely on the baby's father or their families, and most of the others said they would request help from other relatives. The respondents' solutions did not vary significantly according to their ages or with whom they lived at this time.

CHAPTER SUMMARY

The average respondent had used seven different support services during pregnancy and the immediate postpartum period. Medical care, parenting or baby care classes, counseling, public assistance, and sex education were the services she and many of her peers used. The number of different support services used did not vary by the respondent's living arrangement, her family's socioeconomic status, or her past participation in a special school program.

The typical mother's use of many different services at this time did not mean she did not need other kinds of help. Concrete help such as food stamps, WIC, public assistance, and babysitting were what she and the other young mothers in the sample said they needed most.

The typical respondent's extensive need for financial help and other concrete services at the time of the first interview should be a cause for concern on the part of service providers and community planners. It is obvious that, while the adolescent's needs may be fully met during pregnancy, new needs emerge as the young mother and her baby grow older. The needs most readily identifiable by the young teenager are financial, and she is probably most open to receiving help on those. This is not to say that she would not benefit from other services such as counseling, but that her most immediate concerns are financial and will probably only be met by nonfamilial sources of help. Social service providers should be sure that they are not duplicating what help the extended family can already offer, since this would be inefficient and can cause divisiveness within the family unit.

Data from the follow-up interview 18 months postpartum indicate that while some of the average mother's financial needs identified at the first session had been met, others remained, the need for food stamps being the most predominant. The need for sex education and parenting classes also increased during the interval between the two interviews among mothers in the study sample. It may be that the respondents recognized that their families could not supply the information they needed at this time about such matters as cognitive development and discipline, or that they are less willing to depend on them as their children grow older.

Regardless of the explanation, it is obvious that these young teenage parents' unmet needs were largely financial ones during the first few months of the baby's life. Over time, only some of these monetary needs were met. In addition, new needs for specific services such as sex education and parenting classes developed. These trends should lead service providers to evaluate the necessity of delivering additional concrete types of support. The timing of services for maximum impact also deserves considerable attention. For example, instead of promoting child development classes for pregnant girls, greater efforts should be directed toward offering accurate information to young mothers during the baby's second and third years of life, since we know that this is when cognitive deficits begin to appear.

CHAPTER ELEVEN

The Mothers'
Expectations
for the Future

The respondents were asked during the interviews about their expectations regarding education, marriage, childbearing, employment, and living arrangements. Questions about ideal, as well as anticipated or real, goals were posed concerning education and living arrangements, for example, ideal—"If you could have your wish, how far would you like to go in school?" and real—"How far do you think you will actually go in school?" These were included to assess the mother's orientation toward the future, in addition to any compromises she might have already made about the plans she held.

EDUCATION

The educational aspirations of the respondents interviewed twice are displayed in table 31. Almost all said at both times that they hoped to finish high school. Forty percent or more at each session hoped ideally to obtain B.A. degrees but only one out of four actually believed she would be able to realize these plans. The expectations of these young adolescents regarding education are comparable to what other researchers have found among slightly older teenagers [Epstein 1980, Furstenberg 1976].

At the first interview, several months after delivery, the respondents who were interviewed twice had real and ideal educational expectations that were significantly different (p < .001). Sixty-eight percent of the sample wanted to go beyond high school, but only 40% thought they would actually be able to do so. Neither the mother's real nor her ideal expectations at this time differed by her age, race, school status, or the last grade either of her parents had completed. However, both were positively associated with higher levels of self-esteem.

By the time of the follow-up interview, many respondents had modified both their ideal and real expectations considerably (p < .001). Thirty-one

TABLE 31   EDUCATIONAL ASPIRATIONS OF THE RESPONDENTS INTERVIEWED TWICE (N = 143)

	At Interview I		At Interview II	
	Real	Ideal	Real	Ideal
Less than 12th grade	5%	1%	5%	1%
12th grade	55%	31%	54%	43%
Junior college	12%	22%	17%	15%
B.A.	21%	41%	20%	34%
Graduate level	7%	5%	4%	7%

(22%) had lowered their ideal expectations, changing their plans from hoping to go beyond high school to completing just the 12th grade. Nineteen mothers (13%), however, held higher ideal expectations at the follow-up interview than they had at the first session. Most of these had originally planned to finish only high school but now hoped to go further. Twenty-four mothers (17%) had reduced their real expectations from the first to the second interview, changing most often from thinking they would go beyond high school to believing they would not. The reverse was true for 29 respondents (20%).

The differences between the respondents' ideal and real educational expectations at the follow-up interview were statistically significant, as they had been at the first session. Due primarily to a reduction in "ideals," however, the two appear to be becoming more similar over time. At the first interview, 68% ideally wanted to go beyond high school but only 40% thought that they would really be able to do so. By the follow-up interview, 56% hoped to go beyond high school while 42% believed they would actually realize these plans.

At the second interview both the mothers' ideal and real expectations were significantly related to school status then, with more of those still attending school having higher ideal and real aspirations. Their future plans were also positively correlated with higher levels of self-esteem at that time. In addition, a significant association existed between their expectations and their plans for marriage in a way that may be surprising to some: More of those who intended to wed hoped to obtain a B.A. or advanced degree. It should be noted, though, that the respondents' educational expectations at this time were not significantly influenced by the experience of a subsequent pregnancy in the interval between the two interviews, as others have found [Shah et al. 1975, Furstenberg 1976].

MARRIAGE

When the respondents were asked in the first interview whether they thought they would eventually marry, 58% of those who participated in both interviews replied affirmatively. A quarter of this group said they actually had plans for marriage in the near future. The other 42% said they were either unsure about marriage or believed they would never marry.

The mothers were also questioned in the initial session about whether they ever felt they would be better off unmarried. Forty-eight percent agreed then that they sometimes had these feelings, but the other 52% said they did not. Significantly more of the respondents with daughters than those with sons said that they sometimes felt they would be better off unmarried. The respondents' opinions on this issue, however, did not vary in any meaningful way by their ages at the time or their mothers' marital status.

The proportion of the sample expecting to marry increased from the first to the second interview, from 58% to 74%. Another 2% were already married at that time, and the remaining 24% thought they would never marry. More of the white than black respondents intended to wed. The mothers' plans for marriage did not differ significantly by any of the following: age, school status, living arrangements, or the occurrence of a subsequent pregnancy. In all, about 7 out of 10 of the respondents were consistent in the answers they gave at both interviews regarding their marriage intentions (68%). Fifty percent said at both times that they planned to marry, and 18% believed they never would. The opinions of the other 32% varied over time.

Expected Age at the Time of Marriage　At the first interview, 38% of those who planned to marry expected to be 20 or younger when they wed. A comparable group (39%) thought they would be between 21 and 29, and one respondent (1%) assumed she would marry in her 30s. The other 22% expecting to marry did not know when marriage might occur.

By the time of the second interview, 37% of the respondents who still intended to wed had modified their expectations regarding age at marriage. Most expected that they would be older than they had previously thought at the first interview (27%), but a sizable group believed they would be younger (10%). The differences, although interesting, were not statistically significant at the .05 level.

Just 28% said during the second interview that they planned to be married by age 20. Most of the others hoped to wed before 30 (55%), but a sizable group contemplated marriage after that (17%). The respondents' marital expectations at this time varied according to their living arrangements, with more of those living away from their parents than those residing with them hoping to wed by age 20. Their timings for marriage was not significantly influenced by the experience of a subsequent pregnancy.

The Best Age for Marriage　A question regarding the best age for marriage was also included in the initial interview. Nearly a third of the sample (32%) thought it was preferable to marry by age 20. Most of the others (54%)

favored marriages between 21 and 30. A few (4%) selected the mid and late 30s as optimal times. The remaining 10% were unsure. The respondents' answers to this question did not vary according to age but did differ by expected age at the time of marriage. More of those believing a somewhat older age was preferable did not expect they would delay their marriages until then.

Attitudes About Marriage The respondents' attitudes regarding the influence of various factors such as premarital sex or pregnancy on marriage were also investigated at the follow-up interview. As is clear from table 32, most of the sample (80%) believe that a woman's being employed after she is married contributes favorably to the marriage. In contrast, the majority view the impact of a premarital pregnancy or the fact that a woman enters marriage having already had a child by another man as either negative or neutral influences.

On only one issue did their opinions differ significantly by age: More of the younger respondents (14 and 15 at Interview II) than the older respondents (16 and 17) thought that entering a marriage having had a child by another man was harmful rather than helpful. Those planning to marry in the future were also more likely to view this negatively than those not intending to wed.

COMPLETED FAMILY SIZE

During both interviews, the respondents were questioned about the total number of children they wanted to have. Their answers are detailed in table 33 on page 92. At the time of the first interview, the mean number of children they desired was 2.5; at the follow-up, approximately 2.7. Their expectations are very similar to what Gustavus [1978] found among high school seniors.

TABLE 32 ATTITUDES REGARDING MARRIAGE—INTERVIEW II (N = 144)

	Helps	Hurts	Makes No Difference	Don't Know
If a woman has a job after she marries, does that *help* or *hurt* the marriage?	80%	5%	6%	9%
Does it *help* or *hurt* the marriage if a woman has had sexual relations with her husband before they marry?	36%	10%	45%	9%
Does it *help* or *hurt* the marriage if she is pregnant when they marry?	31%	35%	24%	10%
Does it *help* or *hurt* the marriage if she has had a child by another man before getting married?	5%	53%	35%	7%

TABLE 33   TOTAL NUMBER OF CHILDREN DESIRED BY THOSE RESPONDENTS INTERVIEWED TWICE (N = 140)

	At Interview I	At Interview II
Only one child	26%	15%
Two children	51%	46%
Three children	11%	24%
Four or more children	12%	15%

The number of children the respondents said they wanted differed significantly at the two interview times. By the follow-up session, 4 out of 10 mothers had already modified their original expectations to include additional children (38%). Just 14% had reduced the number of children they hoped to have. Plans for the other 48% remained the same.

The respondents' childbearing expectations did not vary significantly at either interview by age, race, or school status, or by the age or sex of their infants. Neither did they differ by the experience of a subsequent pregnancy. The findings regarding race are just opposite to what Bonham and Placek [1978] found among married women they studied nationally; black women in that sample expected more births than white women. It is noteworthy that the younger teenagers in this sample said (about a year and a half after their first births) that they wanted more children than did the older adolescent mothers in Zitner and Miller's [1980] study.

As in this study, Furstenberg [1976] identified a slight increase over time in the ideal number of children desired by the young mothers he surveyed. He determined, however, that many thought they would not actually be able to have the number of children they wanted because of economic constraints. One should keep in mind when considering these results that other research [Westoff et al. 1963, Bumpass and Westoff 1970] has shown that women's predictions for their future fertility were not highly accurate in terms of the actual number of children they eventually had.

Timing of the Next Pregnancy   The respondents who planned to have more children were asked in the follow-up interview when they wanted to become pregnant again. Most selected their early 20s as the best time (60%), but 10% chose their late teens, and 14% their late 20s or 30s. The other 16% intending to have additional children could not say what the best time would be. The respondents' opinions regarding the ideal age for their next pregnancies did not vary significantly by age, race, current use of contraceptive methods, or expectations of exact age at the time of marriage.

Attitudes Toward a Pregnancy in the Next Few Months   During the follow-up interview, the respondents were also questioned about how they would react if they found they were pregnant in the next few months. Of those not currently pregnant, three out of four reported that they would be upset. The other 22% indicated that they would react positively to another pregnancy in the near future. Those who were not sexually active at this time were significantly more likely than those who were to say that they would respond negatively. Mothers who had strong positive attitudes about the acceptability of abortion were also more likely to expect that they would feel negative about becoming pregnant in the next few months (although differences were not significant at the .05 level). The young mothers' expectations regarding their reactions to a pregnancy in the next few months did not vary by their own or the baby's age at that time, race, living arrangements, or whether they were using contraceptive methods.

Ideal Age for Having a First Child Beginning childbearing in adolescence appears to be the preference of most of the young mothers studied even after their own experiences. When interviewed several months after delivery, more than half of the respondents said that the best age for having a first child was before 20 (58%). This included a few mothers who suggested 15 or younger as the ideal age (2% of the total). Most of the others thought that a woman's early or mid 20s was the optimal time to start having children. Although the respondents' opinions regarding the best age for a first birth were significantly correlated with their attitudes about the right time for marriage, two out of five expected the birth prior to the marriage.

EMPLOYMENT STATUS IN FIVE YEARS

At both interviews, almost all of the respondents anticipated that they would be working in 5 years (98% at Interview I, 97% at Interview II). Most aspired to nursing, secretarial, or sales-related vocations. Epstein [1980] also found that a high proportion of the slightly older pregnant adolescent mothers she interviewed expected to be employed in 5 years.

LIVING ARRANGEMENTS IN FIVE YEARS

In the first interview, the respondents were asked two questions about their future living arrangements. One pertained to their ideal expectations— "With whom would you like to be living in five years?" and the other to their

TABLE 34 EXPECTATIONS AT INTERVIEW I FOR LIVING ARRANGEMENTS IN 5 YEARS (N = 176)

	Ideal	Real
Alone with child	35%	53%
With mother (and father for 3 respondents)	12%	14%
With boyfriend/husband	48%	30%
With other maternal relatives	3%	2%
Other	2%	1%

real plans—"With whom do you think you'll actually be living in five years?" Their answers are shown in table 34.

As the table suggests, the mothers' real and ideal expectations were significantly different. More hoped ideally to be living with either their boyfriends or husbands but fewer believed these situations would actually materialize, expecting instead to be living alone with their babies.

Neither the respondents' real nor their ideal expectations regarding their future living arrangements differed significantly by their ages at the time of the first interview. Their real expectations did vary, however, by race, with more of the black than white mothers saying that they thought they would be living with their boyfriends or husbands in 5 years. There were no meaningful racial differences in the respondents' ideal expectations. In the follow-up session, no inquiry was made into the mothers' plans for future living arrangements.

CHAPTER SUMMARY

At both interview times, the average respondent expected to complete at least 12 years of formal education. She wanted ideally to attend college and obtain a B.A. degree, but doubted she would be able to realize her aspirations. During the first 18 months after her baby's birth, she had lowered her educational plans substantially.

The respondent's plans for marriage and childbearing also changed as her baby grew older, like those of many of her peers. The proportion of the sample intending to marry increased from 58% at the first interview to 74% at the follow-up session. The mean number of children desired grew from 2.5 at the first interview to 2.7 at the second. Four out of 10 respondents had altered their expectations over time to include more children.

These changes in the respondents' future expectations are not surprising in view of their ages and level of cognitive and emotional development. However, they do indicate that the mothers are making compromises about their futures at an unrealistically early age. It is possible that an accelerated role change into motherhood may mean that some will never explore, as others do in late adolescence, the wide range of possibilities of what they might become as adults. The time for developing a mature sense of identity will have been distorted by adult responsibilities, and the full consequences of this on the young mothers' emotional development are, as yet, unknown.

CHAPTER TWELVE

Discussion and Concluding Remarks

The preceding chapters have provided a highly detailed description of the lives of these young adolescent mothers from the time they realized they were pregnant through the first year and a half after their babies' births. In many ways, they appear similar to other women who are first-time parents; in other ways, they are quite like typical 12- to 15-year-olds. The reality, however, is that they share characteristics of both groups as they attempt to be children and parents simultaneously. This double role, brought on by an accelerated transition into parenthood, was probably the most consistent theme evidenced during the interviewing and the data analysis phases of this study, as well as through informal reports from the respondents, their parents, service providers, and social agency administrators visited at the three study sites.

In view of the tremendous responsibilities facing very young mothers and the competing requirements on their time and efforts, one might suspect that they would handle the demands of being parents poorly and also be less successful at activities appropriate for young teenagers, such as school or peer relationships. One could also hypothesize that the young adolescents' immaturity would be a hindrance in procuring community services and making well-informed decisions.

While these suspicions are reflected and reinforced by the negative public attitudes prevalent toward adolescent pregnancy and child rearing, the actual data collected for this study did not support an entirely negative view. The majority of the young teenagers interviewed were actually faring quite well in the double roles they pursued through the first 18 months after delivery. This is not to say in any way that the high pregnancy and birth rates for teenagers should be accepted unequivocally or encouraged, or that there are not some specific problems related to early childbearing and child rearing that should be addressed by creative program activities and governmental policies.

⸗ One should be aware, however, that much of the negative public opinion that currently exists regarding adolescent childbearing seems to be attributable to concern over two specific aspects of the problem: high rates of out-of-wedlock births and huge governmental expenditures on the Aid to Families with Dependent Children program, food stamps, and other types of public support needed by young and single parents. Much of the research that has been conducted using samples of pregnant adolescents or young parents has also resulted in reports that focus principally on negative outcomes. Only a small portion of the literature emphasizes the young mothers' strengths and accomplishments. ⸗

The following discussion offers a comprehensive, integrated view of both the positive and negative outcomes of early childbearing for the young adolescents in the sample. Although all of the relevant findings have been presented elsewhere in this report, it is important that they be pulled together in one place so that all aspects of the teenage parents' lives are seen as interrelated, a blend of achievements and difficulties. Only with this perspective can well-informed decisions be made regarding the provision of specific services or promotion of policy alternatives.

The current economic situation and related federal and local policies that have resulted in fewer dollars being available for social services, as well as increased competition for these financial resources, make careful scrutiny of these study findings imperative. No longer can the full array of services be provided simply because a program is already in place, or because of the agency's or an individual professional's preference. Clearly defined goals for adolescent parents, such as high school completion and routine medical checkups at specific intervals, have to be agreed upon by voluntary and public agency service providers and administrators, school officials, health care professionals, religious leaders, and others at the community level, if progress is to be made in minimizing the negative outcomes of early childbearing, maximizing the positive behaviors exhibited by many young mothers, and preventing untimely pregnancies in the first place. Any consensus on these goals at the state and federal levels would, of course, also be highly desirable. Services must be offered to and used by young parents that will result in the achievement of these goals in an effective and efficient manner, avoiding the duplication of support that may already be available from existing community agencies or the informal network of family and friends. Periodic evaluations of service delivery systems should be mandated so that progress toward the attainment of the desired goals can be measured, and, if necessary, modifications in the service plan instituted.

OUTCOMES FOR THE STUDY MOTHERS AND BABIES

Mother's Health Care Overall, most of the respondents did exceedingly well at getting health care for themselves during pregnancy and after delivery. Success in this area is probably explained by the widely accepted importance of quality health care and the vast array of medical services available in these communities. The respondents averaged 11.6 prenatal medical visits, more than those received by the general population who obtain care. Four out of 10 had received 13 or more checkups prenatally, thus meeting the number recommended by the American College of Obstetricians and Gynecologists [1974]. However, the numerous medical appointments are only part of the picture; timing of these services is another. Over half of the sample did not begin prenatal care until the second trimester of pregnancy or later. The actual impact of delaying care is not fully known, since in this study, unlike others with older teenagers, the timing of prenatal care, as well as the number of visits, was not significantly related to obstetrical outcomes such as prematurity and birth weight. Although the data do not support advocacy for additional medical appointments during pregnancy, it is the author's opinion that specific program activities directed to improving the quality of the young mother's overall health care during the prenatal period (i.e., nutrition, exercise) could result in a lower rate of negative obstetrical outcomes. Pregnant adolescents need to be educated about the competing demands that pregnancy and young age place on their bodies. According to Heald [1975], caloric and protein requirements are greatest during the adolescent growth spurt than at any other time of life. The recent General Mills [1979] survey on family health indicates that most teenagers admit they are not well informed about preventive medicine, diet, and nutrition.

Many of those who provide prenatal medical care to young teenagers could also include more information during clinic appointments about nutrition and preventive health care. From the informal reports of the study respondents and social service providers, it appears that a large portion of the obstetricians' and gynecologists' time is spent on the physical aspects of pregnancy (i.e., weight gain, blood pressure). Little emphasis is directed to the young teenager's diet, sleeping and eating habits, use of drugs or cigarettes, or emotional reactions. These latter issues must be seen by physicians and other medical professionals as central rather than peripheral, and adequate time for counseling and information should be allocated at each prenatal care visit, not just at a single appointment. In addition to physicians, psychologists, nurses, paramedics, and midwives, among others, may be valuable sources for providing this type of information to pregnant teenagers. Concrete reminders, such as a prescribed diet or having an adolescent keep a diary of what she eats during a week, may also help the expectant girl as well as the service provider to maximize the chances of positive outcomes in the delivery.

Babies' Health Care   As with their own health care, the respondents were quite successful at getting medical services for their babies. Within their first 18 months, 80% of the children had been taken to a physician for four or more checkups and most had received all the necessary immunizations. However, despite these routine visits, the incidence of health problems such as colds and diarrhea was surprisingly high. Over half of the infants had experienced at least one problem within the first few months after delivery. Nearly a quarter had been hospitalized overnight by the time they were 18 months old. Recurring illnesses were common for 53% at that time. However, even with their infants' health problems, almost all of the mothers indicated that they were satisfied with the health care their children received.

It is clear that the present medical services provided for these babies have to go beyond routine checkups and immunizations and focus on preventive health care and identification of the early signs of illness. Many of the respondents in this sample said that they did not feel competent handling a several-months-old child who is ill or injured. One suggestion for service improvement in this area is to make physicians and health care professionals more aware of the problems and information needs that young parents have. A multidisciplinary team approach to service delivery that would include teachers, social workers, counselors, physicians, nurses, and so forth, would probably be beneficial.

Periodic home visits by public health nurses or specially trained paraprofessionals would also likely result in fewer health problems for the babies, as well as earlier identification of developmental delays and handicaps. This service model exists in the U.S. (as in Manchester, NH at the Visiting Nurse Association—Home Health Agency of Manchester, Inc.) and deserves careful attention. Ideally, such contacts would be mandated by law for mothers under 17 or 18—those who with the baby are considered to be at highest risk of health problems and need for service—until the child enters school. The home health visitors would be able to offer advice and information about a variety of issues: child care and development, how to negotiate the community service system and obtain needed assistance, sex education and contraceptives, and counseling on personal problems. They could also monitor the young mother's progress toward achieving certain goals such as high school completion and prevention of another pregnancy. Close supervision might mean that some negative outcomes of early childbearing could be averted or minimized. For example, if a young mother was absent from school frequently or stopped attending classes altogether, the home visitor would detect this before too much school was missed and could help the young mother return by arranging needed services such as counseling, tutoring, or transportaton, or by facilitating a classroom or school change.

Self-Esteem The self-esteem of the young teenage mothers in the study sample appears moderately high throughout the first year and a half after delivery. Nearly all regard themselves as popular and accepted by others. They believe they value themselves as highly as others value themselves. Since no comparison group was available, the self-esteem of those in the sample relative to that of other young teenagers from similar backgrounds who are not yet pregnant was impossible to ascertain. However, the self-esteem scale used was found to be highly reliable at both interview times, as were the two larger scales from which all but four of the items on this scale were drawn. The few teenage mothers who have low self-esteem, about 10% of the total sample, probably need intensive counseling and a wide variety of support services if they are to cope effectively with the additional responsibilities of parenting and become self-sufficient as adults.

Education As in the areas of health and self-esteem, most of the young teenage mothers fared quite well in continuing in school, with relatively good attendance records. Eighty-five percent were still enrolled at the time of the first interview (several months after delivery) and 69% at the second session (18 months postpartum).

While it is certainly encouraging that 7 out of 10 are going to school a year and a half after their babies' births, the fact that the others have dropped out is cause for great concern. Those who had left school by the first interview tended to be older and white, to have experienced health problems soon after delivery, and to be living away from their parents. The latter may have meant that they had more difficulty arranging regular child care for the 6 or 7 hours each day they need to be in school. Lack of child care and a dislike of school were the major reasons for school discontinuation by the follow-up interview.

The dropout rate of 31% by 18 months postpartum is disturbing in view of the mothers' age and the number of years of high school they still have to finish before obtaining diplomas. Moore et al. [1981] have determined from the National Longitudinal Study of the Labor Market Experiences of Young Women, funded by the U.S. Department of Labor, that by age 24, girls who delivered a baby at age 15 or younger had completed an average of only 9 years of school, while those who had given birth at 16 or 17 had completed 10.5 years. They also emphasize the negative impact that early marriage has on the amount of formal education a woman is able to complete, and that the effects of an early marriage and an early birth are difficult to separate since they often occur together. Even when factors such as family background, educational goals, and age at marriage are controlled statistically, the women who began childbearing at age 15 or younger had completed nearly 2 fewer years of schooling than those who were childless at age 24. In all of the analyses Moore et al. [1981] conducted, age at first birth was the strongest or one of the strongest factors influencing educational attainment. Although some women do manage to return to school or pass equivalency tests, many do not overcome the initial loss over longer periods of time.

Despite the high educational aspirations and the relatively good school attendance of the majority of the young adolescent mothers in the study sample during the first year and a half of the baby's life, the findings of Moore et al., along with the 19% repeat pregnancy rate for the sample and the decrease over time in the proportion attending school, lead one to expect that more of the young mothers will drop out of school in the continuing months because of dissatisfaction with the child care arrangements they have, lack of child care, subsequent pregnancies, difficulties with school personnel, frequent absences, or a dislike of school.

The need for services to further regular class attendance is very great. Currently, most special school activities are available to teenagers only during pregnancy and the first few months after delivery. Although participation in these programs may result in better overall prenatal care (although the number of prenatal care visits was not significantly influenced by special school attendance), more problem-free deliveries and healthier babies, as well as good school attendance during pregnancy, it does not appear to be a major influence in school continuation a year or so later. There is little doubt that special school programs of long duration, preferably through the first few years of the child's life, would help to reduce the dropout rates. However, the costs of separate educational facilities make them somewhat unrealistic to propose. Somehow, young parents must be "mainstreamed" into their community schools after the birth of their babies and receive needed supplemental support services, such as child care and transportation or stipends for family-based child care, until they graduate from high school or pass equivalency examinations.

Klerman and Jekel in 1973 stressed the need for long-term programs: "Programs offering services geared to only the prenatal period and a few postpartum months (crisis intervention) will have short-term impact on school-age mothers" (Klerman and Jekel 1973:130). Despite their warnings, few programs exist that continue into the second and third years of the child's life. Certainly, high school completion for teenage mothers should be at the top of the list of goals agreed upon by service providers, policy makers, and community leaders, second only perhaps to optimal health outcomes for both the young mothers and infants.

School personnel also should be aware and tolerant of the adolescent mother's needs and problems, such as frequent clinic appointments for the baby, so that they can be active promoters of school continuation. Occasional tardiness and absences are to be expected, considering the young mother's many responsibilities. Tutoring and help with school assignments may also be necessary, and well-trained volunteers could be effective in providing this help, as well as serving as advocates for the young mothers in other areas./

It is significant that more than half of the study respondents were receptive about school-based day care as an alternative if their current child care arrangements became unavailable. School administrators should consider providing these services, particularly for young parents whose child is of preschool age and those whose family and friends are no longer able and willing to care for the child.

Although service providers can enhance the teenage parents' chances for school completion, the key to that accomplishment lies within the young parents themselves. They must be made fully aware of the potential direct and indirect consequences of their early parenthood: truncated education, earlier marriage [Moore et al. 1981], marital dissatisfaction and increased chance of dissolution [McCarthy and Menken 19791], more unwanted or unplanned children [Trussell and Menken 1978], welfare dependence [Moore 1978], and less prestigious jobs and less job satisfaction/[Card and Wise 1978]. The media offer vast opportunities for the dissemination of this information to the public. Films such as those developed by the Children's Home Society of California ("Growing Up Together: Four Teen Mothers and Their Babies" and "Teenage Father") that realistically portray the problems and consequences of early parenthood are already available and are very appropriate for use in junior high classrooms, youth groups, and church programs. Panel discussions involving pregnant adolescents, young parents, potential grandparents, and adoptive couples, have also been used effectively at social service agencies such as Florence Crittenton Services in Charlotte, NC to help those who are already pregnant make informed decisions about becoming parents or relinquishing their infants for adoption. The potential for using a similar format in junior high schools, church groups, and recreational programs for those not yet pregnant and/or sexually active has not been realized.

Coupled with these efforts to inform young people of the consequences of untimely births must be the provision of assurances that meaningful adult roles exist for them and that they have control over their futures. Exposure to career opportunities and delineation of the educational and experiential pathways toward acquiring well-paying, stimulating jobs are imperative. Teenagers need to know that merely aspiring to be teachers or nurses will not make it so. Given the high levels of unemployment in the neighborhoods where many young adolescents are living, it is critical that they have positive, successful role models, persons they can emulate and seek out for advice. Only through completion of a high school education and additional training and job acquisition and permanent employment will the high rates of welfare dependency for women who begin childbearing in adolescence be reduced.

Use of Contraceptives   As in the other major outcome areas, most of the young teenage mothers in the study sample are successful in using contraceptives or refraining from intercourse to prevent another pregnancy. Seventy-five percent were using a contraceptive method at the time of the first interview several months after delivery, and 66% were doing so at the follow-up session 18 months postpartum.

While the finding that two out of three are employing contraceptives a year and a half after their first child's birth is certainly positive, it is a cause for great concern that at least 15% are sexually active and not using any form of birth prevention and are thus at a high risk of becoming pregnant again, that there has been a decrease over time in the proportion using contraceptives, that many who employ methods do not use them consistently or correctly, and that one out of five of the young teenagers has already experienced another pregnancy.

One step toward improvement would be to increase public awareness of the prevalence of intercourse among adolescents. Being well acquainted with the facts regarding adolescent sexual activity would most likely result in some adults, particularly parents and relatives, taking more active roles in their children's daily supervision and sex education. While 8 in 10 parents and 6 in 10 teenagers believe that parents should educate their children about contraception [General Mills, Inc. 1976], few would agree that they are effective at this task.

According to some, the provision of accurate, comprehensive sex education at an early age would result in fewer girls becoming sexually active at young ages. Fox and Inazu [1979] have found that, after controlling background variables, mothers of girls who were virgins at 14 and 15 were far more likely to have discussed sex-related topics with their daughters before age 12 than mothers of girls who were no longer virgins. They also determined that the frequency of sex-related communication at this age was related to responses that indicate self-responsible sexual and contraceptive behavior for both those sexually active and those not. Therefore, both the timing of sex education and the range of information offered deserve the careful consideration of parents, teachers, school administrators, and social agency personnel. Obviously, sex education has to encompass more than anatomy and physiology. The less well-charted areas of responsibility and emotional reactions should be addressed. Standards of socially acceptable sexual behavior have to be identified and supported by well-grounded arguments that are appropriate to the age and cognitive abilities of those receiving sex education.

The acquisition of knowledge about human sexuality must be viewed as a life-long process, best begun in the home under parental supervision. It should be only one aspect of the information imparted about total health care, which includes nutrition, preventive health behavior, basic first aid, and hygiene. Since sex education is a life-long process, information must be presented gradually, in ever-increasing levels of complexity. A one-hour discussion with a parent or a 10-week course in school during puberty does not fulfill one's responsibility for helping children understand their sexuality.

Young teenagers certainly need to be better educated regarding the risks of pregnancy. Even after participating in a sex education program and experiencing first births, no more than one in five respondents in the study sample could correctly identify when in the menstrual cycle they were most likely to conceive. Although sex educators in schools or social service agencies appear successful in teaching adolescents about a variety of contraceptive methods, they have difficulty imparting more abstract concepts, such as the risks of pregnancy. Considering young adolescents' cognitive abilities and immature capacity for abstraction, this is not surprising. Better ways have to be found to convey this information (i.e., charting the most fertile periods on a calendar, or discussing other physical signs of the cycle such as weight gain, breast tenderness, and temperature).

But provision of information to adolescents and their parents will not be enough to assure lower birth rates. The dynamics of contraceptive use must also be clearly understood. Luker [1975] has hypothesized that some women take calculated risks in deciding not to use contraceptives. For them the benefits of pregnancy may be considerable or the negative consequences they perceive in using prevention methods may outweigh the positive ones. Service providers and policy makers have to recognize that pregnancy and motherhood provide some teenagers with what they believe are socially acceptable adult roles and proof of femininity and maturity. Young women may also view pregnancy as a way of solidifying their relationships with the baby's father. Unless these girls are provided with other life options they feel they can realistically attain, the situation in which they decide to become pregnant and carry the pregnancy to term, justifying their actions by saying "I'm going to be pregnant sometime anyway, why not now?" will be common.

Another dynamic affecting adolescents' use of contraceptives is that many say they do not employ prevention methods because they do not intend to have intercourse. Zelnik and Kantner [1979] found this to be the most common reason for not using contraceptives. Whether this is due to denial of one's sexual life or merely poor planning because of the irregularity of intercourse, it is obvious that a different approach is needed in providing family planning services to this particular population. Contraceptive technologists, gynecologists, and drug companies have yet to promote a prevention method that is highly suitable for teenagers' sexual habits, lack of privacy, and cognitive immaturity. Certainly a safe, reliable device that could be obtained without a prescription and used after sexual intercourse—a "morning-after pill" deserves careful study. Teenagers may also need concrete reminders to renew prescriptions for birth control pills or to use methods efficiently. In this study sample, several repeat pregnancies might have been prevented if phone calls had been made to remind the respondent to obtain the pills, or if the oral contraceptives had been provided free of charge, or if transportation to the clinic had been available. Contraceptive vigilance for women this age will only occur if incentives for appropriate use are built into the delivery of services, and if disincentives, such as difficulty with transportation and problems arranging appointments, are minimized.

Early use of existing prescription contraceptives, in particular, could also reduce the number of adolescent pregnancies, and this should be encouraged for all women by professionals at family planning clinics, social service agencies, schools, and other community programs, as well as by parents and the media. Zabin [1981] has estimated that if 18- or 19-year-olds who had never used a medically prescribed method started using one within 1 month of initiating intercourse, the risk of conception over a 2-year period could be reduced by 59% from what it would have been if they used no method: "Twenty-seven percent of those who switched to prescriptive methods would become pregnant compared to 66% of the never users" [Zabin 1981:73].

The school environment offers tremendous possibilities for encouraging the use of contraceptives among adolescents. Two successful health clinics already exist in St. Paul, MN high schools, which offer comprehensive medical and counseling services, including venereal disease and pregnancy testing; contraceptive information; and athletic, job, and college physicals. Referrals are made to a local medical center for those interested in obtaining a contraceptive device. A day care center is also available through these programs. Pregnancies in these settings have declined by 40%; fertility by 23% [Edwards et al. 1980]. Eighty-seven percent of the female students who have come for family planning services continued using contraception after 3 years. Edwards et al. emphasize the need for such programs in the junior high schools so that younger adolescents can receive services to help them become sexually responsible and prevent unplanned pregnancies.

School-based programs may also be the best locations for providing services to young males who are often difficult to reach. Typically, approaches to prevent adolescent pregnancies focus primarily on young women. To be truly effective they must also include their male partners. Finkel and Finkel [1975] found in their study of urban male high school students that the last time the students had intercourse, 55% had not used contraceptives or had relied on withdrawal or their partner's douching. Half of those boys had first had sexual intercourse before age 13. This clearly points out the need for targeting sex education to both boys and girls at the junior high school level if the desired outcomes of promoting sexual responsibility and preventing early pregnancies are to be achieved.

Improved availability of contraceptives also should be encouraged, particularly for younger teenagers. This means clinic hours that are compatible with school schedules and privacy requirements, and elimination of restrictive policies such as parental notification and full payment prior to service. Shah et al. [1975] determined that access to contraception was a major problem for 3 out of 10 of all the respondents in their sample who said they had never used contraceptives. This was second only to the adolescents believing they could not become pregnant because of time of the month, their ages, or infrequent sexual activity. Many said they did not know where to go for contraceptives or thought they were too expensive, and a few were not aware that ways to prevent pregnancy existed.

Economic Well-Being The young teenagers' heavy reliance on public assistance and their parents' employment was not unexpected because of their ages and their parents' marital status at the time they were interviewed. Sixty percent were receiving financial support from the government, predominantly AFDC, within several months of giving birth to their first babies. The proportion had risen to 85% a little more than a year later. About half of the respondents also relied on their parents' income at both times. These young adolescent mothers were more likely than the older teenage mothers in Zitner and Miller's [1980] sample to be receiving public assistance at 18 months postpartum.

Although financial self-sufficiency for young mothers is a goal everyone would agree with, it should be strongly emphasized that the route to achieving this goal will be a long one for those aged 12 to 15 at the time of their first births. The direct relationships between the amount of education completed and job attainment and, therefore, income, makes the completion of high school and specialized training imperative. One has to remember, though, that most of the girls in the study sample have 4 or more years of school to finish satisfactorily before obtaining high school diplomas. They need help to attend classes regularly and perform well in school.

Recent increases in the number of demonstration programs aimed at reducing welfare dependency are a positive outcome of public concern regarding adolescent pregnancy and parenting. However, few of these programs have lasted long enough to effect the goals desired. The programs may have to last several years to help the youngest parents, while older teenage mothers who have already completed high school or can pass equivalency examinations with some tutoring can benefit from shorter periods of intensive job training and related counseling. Supplemental services such as child care and transportation may also be needed for mothers of any age to participate in these activities. Community planners and service providers designing such programs must bear in mind age-specific differences among adolescent mothers when selecting their target populations and identifying goals for them.

Project Redirection, funded by the Department of Labor and the Ford Foundation, is one program that shows considerable promise. Operating in five cities, the project serves pregnant teenagers and adolescent mothers aged 17 or younger by linking them with services that support the project's goals: continued schooling; acquisition of employment skills; delay of subsequent pregnancy; and ultimately, economic self-sufficiency [Branch et al. 1981]. Two aspects of the program are particularly noteworthy: comprehensive services provided through a brokerage format, and the "Community Women Component" in which a teenage parent is paired with an older woman who serves as a positive role model and advocate. Since Project Redirection has been in operation for only about 2 years at this writing, an assessment of the program's full impact is not yet available. However, preliminary reports indicate early successes: helping drop-outs return to school or complete their education, increased participation in family planning and sex education activities, better use of pediatric services for the children, and increased attendance at preemployment services and classes in life management [Branch et al. 1981]. Those interested in replicating such a program in their communities should follow the development of Project Redirection, since the program's implementation and impact are being fully assessed and documented.

Competence as Parents and Child's Developmental Status   As the previous discussion of health care indicated, most of the young mothers are successful in acquiring routine medical checkups and necessary immunizations for their infants. However, they seem less competent in preventing their babies' frequent colds and other health problems.

Nine out of 10 respondents were also able to find child care arrangements they thought were satisfactory, and half continued to have the same persons caring for their children through the first year and a half after delivery. Despite the consistency and high levels of expressed satisfaction in these situations at the second interview 18 months postpartum, 45% said they had disagreements with the other caretakers over how things should be done with their babies, and a third said they did not have enough care.

When the children's developmental status was assessed through the mothers' reports on Alpern and Boll's [1972] *Development Profile*, 6 or more out of 10 of the babies were found to be advanced for their ages by at least 2 months in all five areas: physical, self-help, social, academic, and communication. They seemed particularly precocious in self-help and social abilities. Although these findings are certainly encouraging, other research indicates that cognitive deficits among children born to teenage mothers first appear in the preschool years.

These findings, as well as several others detailed below, lead one to suggest changes in the timing of the delivery of parenting education classes for teenage parents, and recommend different intervention strategies for reaching the children. Seventy percent of the young mothers in the sample had been to parenting or baby care classes, most often before delivery. However, despite frequent attendance at such classes and past experiences caring for young children, many said they did not feel competent at tasks such as toilet training or coping with a child who was ill or injured. At the time their babies were 18 months old, they mentioned an average of 2.5 different problems they frequently had, such as getting the baby to eat at mealtimes or behave in a desirable manner.

Even though the respondents had received parenting education, their knowledge of appropriate child development expectations as indicated in their performance on the *Knowledge Scale* [Epstein 1980], was not extensive. However, they did give more correct answers on this scale than one would have expected on the basis of random choices. It should be noted that they were more likely to respond correctly to items related to basic care and physical and motor perceptual development than to items related to cognitive, language, and social development. The number of correct answers the young mothers gave on the *Knowledge Scale* [Epstein 1980] did not differ significantly by their past attendance at parenting education classes or special school programs.

These findings, as well as the fact that half of the sample mothers expressed the need for parenting education at the second interview 18 months postpartum, suggest that there is room for much improvement in this area. Providing parenting education during pregnancy seems ineffective and inefficient. At that time, the pregnant adolescent is more concerned with the developing fetus and her reactions to the pregnancy, not how she will toilet train her baby 2 years later. Emphasis during pregnancy should be placed on nutrition, exercise, and preparation for delivery. After the baby is born, new needs for information and services appear, but this is typically when most comprehensive programs end.

Ideally, parenting education should begin soon after delivery right in the hospital maternity unit and continue until the child enters school. The study data have shown that most of the babies born to the mothers in the sample fare quite well during the first year and a half after delivery. However, other research indicates that cognitive deficits appear as early as the preschool years, making intervention when the children are toddlers especially important.

In addition to improving the timing of parenting education activities, service providers must also become more adept at conveying information about cognitive, social, and language development, as well as other issues involving abstract conceptualization. The young mothers' cognitive immaturity should be kept in mind when curricula are created. We cannot expect these 12- to 15-year-olds to generalize what they have learned from one situation to another without the help of concrete examples, modeling exercises, and routine reminders.

It is important to note here that the young mothers' knowledge of appropriate child development expectations, as evidenced on the *Knowledge Scale* [Epstein 1980], was not a strong predictor of their babies' developmental status. The challenge remains for teachers and social service providers to promote the transfer of what is learned in parenting classes to actual interactions between the young mothers and their babies.

The importance of the other adult caretakers in enhancing the infant's development also should be recognized. Since many other family members care for the child regularly, they would probably also benefit from parenting education to help them create optimal learning environments for the child. Engaging them in programs may be difficult, however, since many think that their vast experience as parents automatically means they are experts on child development. The young mothers' mothers and other relatives will have to be attracted to programs that meet their needs, such as counseling regarding the difficulties of dealing with pregnant daughters or information regarding community services available for young parents. Once involved in such activities, child development and parenting information can be introduced where appropriate. The baby's father may also have to be drawn in through such activities as job training or sports programs.

The Minnesota Early Learning Design (MELD) [1981] is one parenting education model that deserves the attention of those interested in starting new programs or modifying existing ones. Through this self-help peer group approach, first-time parents meet regularly for 40 to 50 2-hour sessions to discuss concerns with one another, as well as with volunteer "facilitators" who are already successful parents and trained in group process skills. Assets of the MELD format are that it is nonthreatening and cost-effective. The comprehensive curriculum focuses on parental concerns at four successive levels in the child's development, beginning in pregnancy and ending when the baby is 2 years old. Parents choose from a wide range of topics that are age-appropriate for their children, and discussion is augmented with films, lectures, and demonstrations. The MELD program has been replicated at many sites across the country in recent years, under the sponsorship of corporations, social service agencies, churches, and neighborhood centers. A special curriculum has also been developed for teenage mothers.

Relationships with Family Members The strengths of the adolescent mothers' families and the support they provide have never been fully recognized or enhanced by social service providers, educators, medical professionals, and others involved in service delivery. Instead, in many cases, the two groups, the formal and informal helping networks, have coexisted in an adversary relationship and often competed with one another in influencing the young mothers' behavior.

The intensive range of help given to teenage parents by their own mothers and other relatives should be acknowledged and encouraged for a variety of reasons: (1) it is generally effective and efficient in reducing the stresses associated with adolescent parenting, (2) duplicating what the families offer would be economically unfeasible, and (3) the teenagers' families are almost always their first sources of help. Persons outside the family are turned to only as other resources are exhausted. The comprehensive long-term support offered by parents and other relatives was certainly evident in this study. Twenty-seven percent of the respondents confided in their mothers after they realized they were pregnant, and another 26% turned to sisters, aunts, cousins, or grandmothers. Throughout the first 18 months following their babies' births, 80% or more of the sample resided with one or both of the parents, and most of the remainder lived with relatives. During the same period, over half of the respondents had mothers who cared for their babies regularly, which allowed many of them to attend school 5 or more hours daily. Most of the others who had someone else caring for their infants routinely relied on sisters or other maternal relatives. Less than one-fifth of the sample depended on nonfamily members for child care.

Family members also played major roles in making decisions regarding the baby, providing emotional support and acting as a source of child development information for the young mother. More than half of the sample said they would consult with their mothers when important decisions had to be made. Eight out of 10 respondents reported that they had relied on their mothers for information about child development either before or after delivery. Many researchers have noted the positive outcomes associated with a moderate amount of familial support, such as adolescent mothers' increased likelihood of finishing high school, being stably employed, and avoiding welfare dependency [Furstenberg 1976]; their less negative relationships with their children as measured by hostile actions, neglect, or maltreatment [Williams 1977]; and their children's higher scores on measures assessing mental development [Stevens 1980]. Epstein [in Sparling 1980] has succinctly summarized the importance of the adolescents' mothers' informal helping network: "Short-term dependence on another adult may be the teenager's best chance for long-term independence."

The reason for drawing attention to the support provided to young adolescent mothers by their families is not to discount the assistance given by the formal service network but rather to make the distinction between the kinds of help given by the two sources. Except for monetary help obtained through public assistance, food stamps, and the WIC food supplement program, most community services for teenage parents end soon after delivery. Following their babies' births, the young mothers rely on their families for all types of help and depend on their communities mainly for the welfare grants and other financial help for which they are eligible.

These patterns of service availability and use clearly point up the need for community agencies to provide the young mother with what her own family is unable to offer: concrete assistance such as money, transportation, job training and placement, food, clothing, and specialized classes in parent education. These are the unmet needs the adolescent mothers themselves identify and express the greatest interest in. Those involved in planning the delivery of services should take careful note of what the sample respondents are telling us about their needs, since these are the areas in which they would be most amenable to receiving help.

There is another reason for the importance of certain community support services. Although a moderate amount of assistance from family members and friends (a "sharing style") may be helpful to the young mother in terms of child care, parenting information, help with personal problems, and so forth, and beneficial to the infant as well [Epstein 1980], too much assistance may be problematic: Stevens [1980] has determined that a very dense and close-knit social network is negatively related to the mental development of infants born to teenagers.

CONCLUDING REMARKS

All the findings from this study and the related discussion lead one to wonder whether the problems of adolescent pregnancy and parenting are not as bad as one had originally thought, or are actually worse. The fact that two-thirds or more of the adolescents giving birth at age 12 to 15 were doing quite well at 18 months postpartum in desired outcomes agreed upon by many—school continuation, contraceptive use or abstinence from sexual intercourse, routine medical care for themselves and their babies, average or advanced developmental status for the infants, financial stability, stable living and child care arrangements, and a moderately strong informal helping network—is cause to believe that, in many ways, much has been accomplished in alleviating the stresses associated with early childbearing. Since success in one area is often highly correlated with positive outcome in another, the fact that one out of three young mothers is not faring well in many of the foregoing areas, coupled with the additional negative findings that appear when one takes a broader view of the lives of the young mothers and their babies—the persistent health problems for both the adolescents and their infants despite regular medical checkups, frequent school absences by many mothers, conflicts with those who regularly care for the baby over how things should be done, inconsistent or inappropriate use of contraceptive methods, and lack of a positive future orientation—lead one to conclude that there is still much to be done.

The following general conclusions from this research project are offered as suggestions for modifications in existing service programs and for new approaches developed as communities direct their efforts toward the problems of adolescent pregnancy and parenting

- Age-specific differences within adolescence must be understood and respected, and the different consequences of unplanned pregnancies or births for various age groups, such as the younger teenager's greater chance of bearing premature and low-birth-weight babies and greater likelihood of increased dependence on her family, must be considered in policy development and service delivery.

- To have a long-term impact on the lives of pregnant adolescents, young mothers, and their children, services must continue for a longer time after delivery, preferably at least until the children enter school.

- Programs for pregnant teenagers and young mothers should focus their limited resources on clearly defined, agreed-upon goals, such as high school completion, adequate medical care and nutrition, stable child care and living arrangements, and so forth. All programmatic activities should be directed toward objectives aimed at meeting these goals. Only by a systematic approach to service delivery will unproductive service efforts be eliminated and progress toward the identified goals be achieved most efficiently and effectively.

- The pregnant teenager's or young mother's extended family (often including the baby's father) is her first source of support and must be recognized and respected. Social service providers' efforts should be directed toward enhancing what the family already provides or offering what the family cannot, instead of duplicating assistance that is already available. The positive behaviors and strengths of teenage parents have to be acknowledged and built upon. Few people are giving these young mothers the positive reinforcement, encouragement, and praise for handling a variety of demands and responsibilities fairly well.

Eleanor Holmes Norton recently called adolescent parenting "the single most important problem confronting the black community today" [quoted in Raspberry, *Los Angeles Times* 1981]. She said, "Ordinarily, young people are expected to provide the group with a fresh start. But what kind of fresh start can there be for us when half the next generation will consist of children who were raised by children?" As the rates of premarital sexual activity and fertility among unmarried white teenagers continue to increase as they have for blacks, there is no doubt that this is a problem transcending race.

The prospect of a large proportion of the children of the next generation being raised by children poses fundamental questions about future child rearing in our nation and about the ability of those future children to cope with and contribute to an ever more demanding and competitive society. That prospect should compel us to examine further the factors leading to the high rate of teenage childbearing, the present and anticipated needs of this special population of youths, and the relationship of the high rate of teenage childbearing to other social and economic problems (e.g., truancy, curtailed education, joblessness, and social service dependency).

The problem of teenage childbearing has broad implications. It cannot simply be wished away. We must face it; we must study it; and we must develop programs that effectively address it. Only by doing so can we help those children who become parents at an early age to handle the simultaneous, competing demands of being both adolescents and parents. Only by doing so can we ensure the best possible development of the infants born under these circumstances. Only by doing so can we hope to encourage future parents to delay childbearing until they reach a level of maturity capable of assuming the emotional, intellectual, and financial responsibilities of being parents. Only in this way can the present generation expect the "fresh start" that each new generation should provide.

REFERENCES

Alan Guttmacher Institute. *Teenage Pregnancy: The Problem That Hasn't Gone Away*. New York: The Alan Guttmacher Institute, 1981.

Alpern, G. D., and Boll, T. J. *Developmental Profile Manual*. Psychological Development Publications, P. O. Box 3198, Aspen, CO 81611, 1972.

American College of Obstetricians and Gynecologists. *Standards for Obstetric-Gynecologic Services*. Chicago, IL: American College of Obstetricians and Gynecologists, 1974.

Baldwin, W., and Cain, V. S. "The Children of Teenage Parents." *Family Planning Perspectives* (January/February 1980): 34–43.

Bane, M. J.; Lein, L.; O'Donnell, L.; Stueve, C. A.; and Wells, B. "Child-Care Arrangements of Working Parents." *Monthly Labor Review* (October 1979): 50–56.

Bayley, N. *Bayley Scales of Infant Development*. New York: Psychological Corporation, 1969.

Bonham, G. S., and Placek, P. J. "The Relationship of Maternal Health, Infant Health and Sociodemographic Factors to Fertility." *Public Health Reports* 93 (May-June 1978): 283–292.

Branch, A., and Quint, J., with Mandel, S., and Russell, S. S. *Project Redirection: Interim Report on Program Implementation*. New York: Manpower Research Demonstration Corporation, 1981.

Briggs, R. et al. "Pregnancy in the Young Adolescent." *American Journal of Obstetrics and Gynecology* 87 (August 1962): 436–441.

Broman, S. H. "Longterm Development of Children Born to Teenagers," in *Teenage Parents and Their Offspring*, edited by K. Scott, T. Field, and E. Robertson. New York: Grune and Stratton, 1981, 195–224.

Bumpass, L. L., and Westoff, C. F. *The Later Years of Childbearing*. Princeton, NJ: Princeton University Press, 1970.

Cannon-Bonventre, K., and Kahn, J. "The Ecology of Help-Seeking Behavior Among Adolescent Parents." Executive Summary (for ACYF Grant No. 90-C-1342). Cambridge, MA: American Institutes for Research, January 1979.

Card, J., and Wise, L. "Teenage Mothers and Teenage Fathers: The Impact of Early Childbearing on the Parents' Personal and Professional Lives." *Family Planning Perspectives* 10,4 (1978): 199–205.

Chilman, C. S. *Adolescent Sexuality in a Changing American Society: Social and Psychological Perspectives*. Bethesda, MD: U. S. Department of Health, Education, and Welfare, Public Health Service, NIH, NICHD, Center for Population Research, 1979.

Coates, J. B., III. "Obstetrics in the Very Young Adolescent." *American Journal of Obstetrics and Gynecology* 108 (September 1970): 68–72.

Coopersmith, S. *The Antecedents of Self-Esteem*. San Francisco, CA: W. H. Freeman & Co., 1967.

DeLissovoy, V. "Child Care by Adolescent Parents." *Children Today* 2 (July-August 1973): 22–25.

Development Associates, 2924 Columbia Pike, Arlington, VA 22204. Private communication with N. Jaffie regarding the evaluation of the Child and Family Resource Program, December 23, 1981.

Educational Testing Service. *Preschool Inventory*. Princeton, NJ, 1970.

Edwards, L. E.; Steinman, M. E.; Arnold, K. A.; and Hakanson, E. Y. "Adolescent Pregnancy Prevention Services in a High School Clinic." *Family Planning Perspectives* 12 (January/February 1980), 6–14.

Epstein, A. S., Ph. D. *Assessing the Child Development Information Needed by Adolescent Parents with Very Young Children*. Final Report. Grant No. 90-C-1341. Ypsilanti, MI: High/Scope Educational Research Foundation, January 1980.

Finkel, M. L., and Finkel, D. J. "Sexual and Contraceptive Knowledge, Attitudes and Behavior of Male Adolescents." *Family Planning Perspectives* 7 (Nov./Dec. 1975): 256–260.

Fox, G. L., and Inazu, J. K. "The Effect of Mother-Daughter Communication on Daughter's Sexual and Contraceptive Knowledge and Behavior." Detroit, MI: The Merrill Palmer Institute. A working paper presented at the annual meeting of the Population Association of America, Philadelphia, PA, April 1979.

Furstenberg, F. F., Jr.; Lincoln, R.; and Menken, J., eds. *Teenage Sexuality, Pregnancy, and Childbearing*. Philadelphia, PA: University of Pennsylvania Press, 1981.

Furstenberg, F. F., Jr. *Unplanned Parenthood: The Social Consequences of Teenage Childbearing*. New York: MacMillan, 1976.

General Mills, Inc. *The General Mills American Family Report 1978–79. Family Health in an Era of Stress.* Minneapolis, MN: Yankelovich, Skelly and White, Inc., 1979.

Gordon, C. "Social Characteristics of Early Adolescence." In *Twelve to Sixteen: Early Adolescence,* edited by J. Kagan and R. Coles. New York: Norton, 1972, 25–54.

Green, L. W. "Manual for Scoring Socioeconomic Status for Research on Health Behavior." *Public Health Report* 85 (September 1970): 815–827.

Gustavus, S. "The Family Size Preferences of Young People: A Replication and Longitudinal Study." *Studies in Family Planning* 4 (1978): 335–342.

Hayghe, H. "Marital and Family Characteristics of Workers—March 1977." *Monthly Labor Review* (February 1978): 51–54.

Heald, F. P. "Adolescent Nutrition." *Med. Clin. N. Am.* 59 (1975): 1329.

Hollingshead, A. B. *The Two-Factor Index of Social Position.* Privately published. 1965 Yale Station, New Haven, CT, 1957.

Klerman, L. F., and Jekel, J. F. *School-Age Mothers: Problems, Programs and Policy.* Hamden, CT: Shoe String Press, 1973.

Luker, K. *Taking Chances: Abortion and the Decision Not to Contracept.* Berkeley, CA: University of California Press, 1975.

Marecek, J. *Economic, Social and Psychological Consequences of Adolescent Childbearing: An Analysis of Data from the Philadelphia Collaborative Perinatal Project.* Final report. NICHD, September 1979.

McCarthy, J., and Menken, J. "Marriage, Remarriage, Marital Disruption and Age at First Birth." *Family Planning Perspectives* 11 (January/February 1979): 21–30.

Minnesota Early Learning Design, 123 East Grant Street, Minneapolis, MN 55403, 1981.

Moore, K. A.; Hofferth, S. L.: Wertheimer, R. F.; Waite, L. J.; and Caldwell, S. B. "Teenage Childbearing: Consequences for Women, Families and Governmental Expenditures." In *Teenage Parents and Their Offspring,* edited by K. G. Scott, T. Field, and E. Robertson. New York: Grune and Stratton, 1981.

Moore, K. "Teenage Childbirth and Welfare Dependency." *Family Planning Perspectives* 10 (1978): 233–235.

Mussio, T. "Primigravidas Under Age 14." *American Journal of Obstetrics and Gynecology* 84 (August 1962).

National Center for Health Statistics. *Monthly Vital Statistics Report. Advance Report Final Natality Statistics, 1978* 29, 1, Supplement (April 28, 1980).

National Center for Health Statistics. *Monthly Vital Statistics Report. Advance Report Final Natality Statistics, September 29, 1981* 30, 6, Supplement (2).

National Center for Health Statistics. Personal communication with Ken Keppel of the Natality Division regarding unpublished data, Annual Report 1979, December 7, 1981.

National Center for Health Statistics. *Vital Statistics of the United States, 1960* 1, *Natality*, 1962.

Nie, N.; Hull, C.; Jenkins, J.; Steinbrenner, K.; and Bent, D. *SPSS: Statistical Package for the Social Sciences.* 2nd ed. New York: McGraw-Hill, 1975.

Piaget, J. *The Origins of Intelligence in Children.* New York: International Universities Press, 1952.

Placek, Paul J., and Taffel, Selma, M. "One Sixth of 1980 U.S. Births by Cesarean Section." *Public Health Reports* 97 (March-April 1982): 183.

Placek, Paul J., and Taffel, Selma M. "Demographic Variation in Cesarean Section Delivery Rates: United States, 1970–1978." Hyattsville, MD: National Center for Health Statistics, DHHS Pub. No. (PHS) 80-1120.1, 1980.

Presser, H. "Early Motherhood: Ignorance or Bliss." *Family Planning Perspectives* 6 (Winter 1974): 8–14.

Querec, L.J., and Spratley, E. *Characteristics of Births, United States, 1973–1975.* DHEW No. (PHS) 78-1908. United States Department of Health, Education and Welfare, Public Health Services, Vital and Health Statistics, Series 21, No. 30, Sept. 1978.

Raspberry, William. "Disaster for the Future." *Los Angeles Times*, October 30, 1981.

Rosenberg, M. *Society and Adolescent Self-Image.* Princeton, NJ: Princeton University Press, 1965.

Ross, S. (Project Director). *The Youth Values Project.* The Population Institute and the State Communities Aid Association, 1979.

Shah, F.; Zelnik, M; and Kantner, J.F. "Unprotected Intercourse Among Unwed Teenagers." *Family Planning Perspectives* 7 (January/February 1975): 39–44.

Sparling, J., ed. *Information Needs of Parents with Young Children: A Synthesis of 15 Child Development Information Research Studies from the Administration for Children, Youth, and Families.* Chapel Hill, NC: Frank Porter Graham Child Development Center, University of North Carolina at Chapel Hill, June 1980.

SRI International. *An Analysis of Government Expenditures Consequent on Teenage Childbirth.* Prepared for Population Resources Center, Menlo Park, CA, April 1979.

Stevens, J.H., Jr. "Teenage Mothers' Social Networks and Black Infant Development." Paper read at Southeastern Conference on Human Development, Alexandria, VA, April 1, 1980.

Trussell, J., and Menken, J. "Early Childbearing and Subsequent Fertility." *Family Planning Perspectives* 10,4 (1978): 209–218.

U.S. Bureau of the Census. *Household and Family Characteristics: March 1979, Current Population Reports, Population Characteristics*, Series P-20, No. 352, issued July 1980a (U.S. Department of Commerce).

U.S. Bureau of the Census. *Supplementary Report—Population and Households by State and Counties, 1980*b (PC 80-51-2).

U.S. Department of Health, Education and Welfare, Social Security Administration, Office of Policy. *Aid to Families with Dependent Children, A Chartbook*, 1979.

Ventura, S.J. National Center for Health Statistics. *Monthly Vital Statistics Report* 26, 5 (September 8, 1977).

Westoff, C.F.; Potter, R.G., Jr,; and Sagi, P.C. *The Third Child*. Princeton, NJ: Princeton University Press, 1963.

Williams, P.R. "Black Illegitimacy and Social Response." A research report prepared in connection with Contract #N01-HD-52825, May 12, 1977.

Zabin, L.S. "The Impact of Early Use of Prescription Contraceptives on Reducing Premarital Teenage Pregnancies." *Family Planning Perspectives* (March/April 1981): 72–74.

Zabin, L.S., and Clark, S.D., Jr. "Why They Delay: A Study of Teenage Family Planning Clinic Patients." *Family Planning Perspectives* 13 (September/October 1981): 205–217.

Zabin, L.S.; Kantner, J.F.; and Zelnik, M. *Family Planning Perspectives* 11 (July/August 1979): 215–22.

Zellman, G.L. *The Response of the Schools to Teenage Pregnancy and Parenthood*. Santa Monica, CA: The Rand Corporation, 1981.

Zelnik, M. "Second Pregnancies to Premaritally Pregnant Teenagers, 1976 and 1971." *Family Planning Perspectives* 12 (March/April 1980):69–75.

Zelnik, M. "Sex Education and Knowledge of Pregnancy Risk Among U.S. Teenage Women." *Family Planning Perspectives* 11 (November/December 1979): 355–357.

Zelnik, M., and Kantner, J.F. "Sexual Activity, Contraceptive Use and Pregnancy Among Metropolitan-Area Teenagers: 1971–1979." *Family Planning Perspectives* 2 (September/October 1980): 230–237.

Zelnik, M., and Kantner, J.F. "Reasons for Nonuse of Contraception by Sexually Active Women Aged 15–19." *Family Planning Perspectives* 11 (September/October 1979): 289–296.

Zelnik, M., and Kantner, J.F. "Attitudes of American Teenagers Toward Abortion." *Family Planning Perspectives* 7 (March/April 1975): 89–91.

Zitner, R., and Miller, S.H. *Our Youngest Parents*. New York: Child Welfare League of America, 1980.